D1234491

YOU ONLY HAVE TO GET RICH ONCE

YOU ONLY
HAVE TO
GET RICH
ONCE

BY

WALTER K. GUTMAN

NEW YORK

E. P. DUTTON & CO., INC.

1961

To Dorothy Darrow
And all pretty things including gold.

Acknowledgments

To David T. Bazelon for assistance on Chapter ten and June Herman who did the editing.

Simon and Schuster, Inc., New York, New York, for permission to quote from *The Sophisticated Investor* by Burton Crane, copyright 1959.

Contents

YOU ONLY HAVE TO GET RICH ONCE

You Only Have to Get Rich Once

This book is intended to be a "how it was done" book rather than a "how to do it." Therefore, there is much looking to history—personal and general.

It is also intended for those who have done it as much as for those who want to do it. Wealth is an occupation just as painting or writing—if you have money you are interested in its various involvements and this book is about these, or at least some of them. If my father had been poor I might never have become interested in the market and I don't know what I might have done. It was because he had some money that I went to a private school. And it was because of the demands and ambitions of an English teacher that I experienced, very early, the thrill of being published. Furthermore, if my mother, whose family had had money but had spent it, had not married someone like my father, she would not have at various times continued with her painting. And if she had been a hard-working scrubwoman I might never have become interested in art. So you can't tell what money will bring you or what it may have deprived you of. Money is a mystery and people who have it don't entirely understand their relationship to it. It is one of those things which can be talked about endlessly.

This is one of the reasons why I became a successful writer for a large Wall Street brokerage house. People who have money, as well as those who want to get it, like to ponder this mystery either directly in conversation or indirectly in someone's writing. If I had been a successful novelist or magazine writer, I naturally would never have written for a broker, but the sort of mystery which writers usually are involved in I somehow did not penetrate sufficiently—except the mystery of art.

In the early 1930's I was one of the recognized art critics of the country. Among other things I wrote the first aesthetic appraisal of what were then called "the talkies"—in other words, the introduction of sound into moving pictures. This was published in *Creative Arts* in 1929 and republished in *The Provincetown Review* in 1960. But it was hard to make a living writing art criticism, especially when most of the magazines folded during the great depression of the Thirties. I lived quite a few years as an impecunious writer and then got tired of it. There is a big gap between this and the time I became a Wall Street writer, but that does not concern this book. The thing that made me noted in Wall Street was not really my long effort as a writer or my innate ability, but that I finally became sufficiently involved in mystery. The usual great mystery of writing is love, and had I been sufficiently involved in this, I would have become some sort of usual professional writer. Had I been involved enough in the mystery of art, I would have, despite everything, continued as an art critic the way others did. Wall Street was where I found the mystery that I became sufficiently involved in to really become a writer. Writing is always about mystery—a textbook is about something that is mysterious to the student. A great writer is one who has a feeling about a great mystery—he penetrates far into it and describes it but he does not solve it. If he tries to, he becomes a philosopher, and if he succeeds, he becomes a scientist. An artist is concerned with existences, and something that is solved is something that is in some way over. Whenever mystery fully ends, existence ends, and the thing that a great artist does is not only to explore mystery and elucidate it but also to create more of it. A great artist not only describes but creates experience. What I did in Wall Street was to find more mystery than was thought to be there and for my readers create more of it.

There are many people in Wall Street who do not understand what I have done. I would say that none of my employers entirely understood it and I don't know that I did either, prior to writing this . . . so whether they understood it or not, or whether it is important, or they or anyone else cares, including myself, whether I care as the years go by, the fact is that I owe Wall Street this thing—that I found mystery there—and also fortune. Wall Street was not my love but it made me successful. It was like getting involved with a woman whom you don't particularly like, but who nevertheless was the right woman for you.

I felt when I failed to establish myself among the professional writers that a writer must take whatever opportunity he has to write regardless of whether it was expected of him. The Stock Exchange itself eventually got annoyed at this because it felt that a Market Letter was not really a proper place to practice literature. A Market Letter, they felt, should be confined to the market. But the investing public liked what I wrote—requests for the letter poured in every week, and the staff hired by my employers to process the returns from their advertising had to work long hours overtime. So this excitement was a real thing—as real as the money. Everybody had always felt the excitement—the customers watching the ticker tape, the newspaper editors who gave the stock market a place on their front pages. But everyone felt they had to be practical about it—that they had to confine the words which they used to express their excitement to descriptions of profit and loss. They thought this because they felt that money was the thing they were excited about. They didn't realize that money was the thing which came out of this excitement. My contribution as a writer was to make them feel, at least somewhat, the excitement that they really had—the true excitement of which money was only the most shining part. In expressing the excitement of the market, I wandered far from the ticker tape—I rambled on about art and women, and psychoanalysis, and when I financed a short *avant garde* moving picture based on a play by Jack Kerouac, I met the most vivid group of people I had ever met in my life, and I wrote about them. And since these brilliant people were those who gave the name "Beat" to the beat generation, I naturally was looked at more suspiciously than ever by the Governors of the New York Stock Exchange, and they wouldn't let me in when I applied to be a member. But while my letters were very strange for a Wall Street Market Letter (or as John Brooks who did a profile of me in *The New Yorker* called them—tip sheets), they brought in the customers. This enthusiasm was not all because of literature. I'm right quite often about the market and about particular stocks—generally the customers make money and get some reading matter too. Looked at this way, I provide the cheapest literature there is.

The first time I felt that the stock market was for me was in 1931, when it was collapsing. My father's fortunes were collapsing too. He wasn't on margin. He owned all of what was considered a diversified portfolio of good, sound stocks and bonds, but they were all collapsing. The magazines I wrote for were collapsing also. Albert Boni, in final payment for what I had done on the staff of *Creative Arts*, gave me a set of Proust. The Gutman family would have been flat as a pancake had not a passionate order clerk said, "Sell out, sell out, they're going lower." I was too innocent to argue. I felt his emotion and I sold. Eight months later what we had owned was worth one-fifth of what I had sold the stocks for, even though when I sold them they were far, far under what they had been a year before. Many conservative people like my father had not been particularly hurt in 1929. It was the collapse from 1931 through 1933 which ruined them.

I bought back at the bottom in 1932—it was one of those innocent moments of luck.

The money we began to make as stocks left their bottom convinced me that Wall Street was better than writing—at least for art magazines—and I did not do any intensive writing for ten years when I joined the research staff of a large brokerage house—Goodbody and Company. In the meanwhile I had had moments when innocence did not lead to profits. There is more to Wall Street than luck, and also more to it than science.

When luck ran out, I began to study seriously—especially in 1938 when the luck that drained out surprised not only me but practically everybody, including the government. Then for a while I applied science too much, for the natural spontaneous thing which thrilled me when I first got down there—and to which the order clerk, Henry Katov, responded to as part of a barometer responds to a change of the atmosphere—cannot be entirely understood. It was not for many years that my innocence came back enough and was well mixed with science. I cannot say that because I picked the bottom of the 1957 market and predicted the revival of 1958–59 and that because I grew cautious in late 1959 and then predicted the election of Kennedy, and with this election, better times, that I have some sort of scientific grip on the situation—those would be fatal last words—but I will say that I eventually reached a blending of naïveté and knowledge which makes a professional; a good practitioner of any art.

As I thought about my experiences and wrote this book, it occurred to me one day that the essence of the whole thing is that you only have to get rich once. You can get rich two or three times if you want to, and avid money makers keep on getting richer, but that is not the essence of being rich. When I met in my youth some other youngsters, usually a girl, from an aristocratic family in Europe, or an old family in New England, I used to wonder how wealth and position were retained so long. Because they were not particularly bright or stupid—they were just pleasant people. The remarkable thing about them wasn't their personalities but the fact that wealth had been with them so long—through wars, sometimes through revolutions—and I concluded that once you have it you can keep it unless you are a fool or gripped by some extravagant passion, or are particularly unfortunate—but to do this you do have to get rich once.

Most people who are rich don't realize how easy it is to keep it, providing they can live within the context of their wealth. One of the most famous books on the stock market is *The Battle for Investment Survival*. I have known the author since before World War II, and I never saw him when he wasn't winning at least a skirmish—but perhaps he didn't feel that way. I have never known anyone who had gotten rich once who, if he managed his fortune prudently, didn't stay that way. There were moments, as in 1932, when they were scared—but relatively speaking even then they were wealthy.

But this getting rich once and coasting thereafter does not particularly appeal to men—I'm sure that if some man who reads this book gets rich, he'll just try to get richer. Women seem more suited psychologically to enjoy the actuality of wealth. There is a relationship between them and things which is very deep, and there is a relationship between wealth and things which is also deep. While women don't need wealth to enjoy a life of deep existence they can use it to glorify, enhance, and dramatize the deep experience with existence that they feel. Men do not have this type of experience with existence—wealth also dramatizes an experience that they have, but they must always go on from wherever they are, whereas women can enjoy where they are. The attraction that men and women have for each other comes from the discovery, lit by brilliant lights at times, of the different existence that each has led and leads. If women could persuade men to be happier with existence, then this principle that you only have to get rich once would be more meaningful. There seems to be one group of men who are happy with existence—these are generals—and I should add prize fighters. A man who is a hero doesn't have to be a hero over again, and if men could learn to have a hero's satisfaction with wealth, then this phrase—"you only have to get rich once"—would have a philosophical as well as practical value. This book doesn't really tell you how to do this—it tells you about some of my experiences with the problem and about the experiences of others; it gives a few practical hints; it describes how during my lifetime, getting rich once has become conspicuously easier than it used to be; and it holds out the candle of hope that with each passing year and the multiplication of technically fostered international wealth, it is bound to be easier still.

PART I

CHAPTER ONE

People Always Feel Rich

When we are young we all feel rich. Happiness or excitement comes with very little money. And when we are old we are still rich. Anyone who has children has had not a few, but many utterly priceless moments. I would rather see my daughter dance than watch Maria Tallchief. There are intimate moments, sudden inventions, and glimpses of a movement so utterly surprising and sweet which can only be had from one's own daughter or from a child of one's friend in the very intimate surroundings of a home.

These are common and ageless experiences, but because they are not translated into money they are never included in economic thinking. When Marie Tallchief dances, the price of the ticket becomes part of Gross National Product. Her salary becomes part of Disposable Personal Income. But when my daughter dances, or my wife cooks, it is not reflected in economic statistics. Yet it is part of life and the feeling of richness.

The feeling of richness has profound and complex effects on practical economics. The feeling of richness is one reason people do not always want money, and do not respond to the profit motive as they are supposed to. For instance, a woman was left a large fortune by an English relative. The will required that she and her family move to England and live there in order to get the benefit of the fortune. She turned down the wealth. She had a greater feeling of richness in America with less money.

If we were purely logical about wealth, and if wealth to us were entirely composed of those types of goods and services which can be evaluated by money, we would all move to some place where at the moment business is booming. Especially where taxes are low, where profit margins for enterprising businessmen are customarily high, and where untapped raw material resources are immense. But very few of us are likely to move. Our life among our familiar surroundings, even with very high taxes, with growing government controls, is still so full of richness that few of us want to leave.

America has received more immigrants than any other nation. The possible financial benefits of moving to America from Europe or Asia in the days of free immigration were more obvious and better advertised than such benefits ever will be again. A world-wide, efficient, experienced mechanism for moving people to America grew up during the decades of mass immigration. Yet even so only 38,000,000 people came to our shores between 1830 and 1914. For every European who came to America during the 83 years of active immigration, at least 40 or 50 lived out their lives in Europe.

The fact that people are so rich, that nature gives them such vast resources of emotional satisfaction means that businessmen must add to this natural feeling of richness if they are to conduct a successful business. This is a basic principle of business success and there are many well-known examples of it. When businessmen give people an increased sense of richness, then people become interested in money. Money is important in a society where it increases the feeling of wealth. Instead of saying the fundamental objective of the businessman is to make money, it might be more significant to say it is his job to make money seem important.

A good investment can be thought of as one in a business which accentuates a feeling of richness for someone—a consumer, a businessman, a political or military leader, a priest. Building cathedrals was once an outstandingly good business. A growth industry is one which is adding spectacularly to some customer's feeling of richness; a non-growth industry is one that is no longer so important in adding to the feeling of richness. All the so-called cyclical industries—copper, steel, automobile, railroads—were once growth industries.

One of the outstanding examples of a business success during my youth was Woolworth. He had made a dime important. All of us of my age have spent pleasant, redolent hours in Woolworth's and other variety chain stores. When we married during the depressed 1930's, those were the places we went to buy bright, colored, useful things for the young household.

During the years when stores of this type were giving people an increased sensation of richness, the stocks of the variety chains were looked upon as growth issues. Not only were the goods on display constantly amazing in their rich values, but the surroundings in which they were purchased became, through the years, more and more delightful.

The shopper's delight in the five-and-ten-cent store was replaced to some extent by the delight in the supermarket. For a while, each year the supermarket became a more marvelous place to shop. One day my wife noticed that we were eating sweet pickles imported from Holland and bought at the First National supermarket. Years ago, such imported specialties were bought only at very exclusive emporia such as Charles or the Vendome. I notice that women go to the supermarkets, not just because the prices may be relatively low—this was once the sole reason for entering the hurly-burly of the early supermarkets—but for the sheer excitement of casting their eyes over the enormous variety of goods on display.

The supermarket has become a place of richer experience as new techniques of packaging have been developed and especially, of course, as new techniques of freezing have developed. This reminds us of the stocks of companies which make packaging materials such as cellophane, polyethylene, and polystyrene, or which extrude them or print on these new materials, or which make frozen fruit juices or instant coffees, etc.

The supermarkets have not produced so great an increase in richness as the variety chains. The old-fashioned grocery store with its assiduous clerks, its talkative butcher, its fragrant smells coming out of the none-too-tight lids of barrels and bins, was a place of considerable charm. The development of the supermarket, at least in its recent phases, has not been as important to the investor as the development of the variety chain, but still the supermarket is a good example of what business is always trying to accomplish—a more comprehensive relationship between the innate feeling of wealth and those material forms of wealth which can be accounted for by business: in other words, the transfer of the natural wealth of feeling into the economic wealth of business. A business becomes richly successful, investors become wealthy as some new technique or concept is able to translate some of the innate natural feelings of richness into commercial forms of richness.

When TV was unveiled, no economist and no businessman, not even the most enthusiastic, had any idea that it would grow like an explosion. Sober-minded people naturally thought that the sets were much too high-priced to appeal to a wide public. They predicted a gradual year-by-year increase in demand as the sets came down in price. But these sober-minded people belonged to an intellectual and moneyed class whose richness of experience would not be greatly increased by television. They had already seen ballets, been to theaters, watched all sorts of big-league performances. It was they, not the public, who didn't want to pay the high prices for the early sets even if they could afford it.

The public felt differently. TV let the public in on experiences which the mass of people had always heard about but had never had a chance to see. It brought a richness of experience which was in line with the price of the sets.

If economists had understood that a market for a new product is created by the value of the product in terms of richness of experience in relation to the price, rather than the price itself, they would not have been so surprised. The truth is that economic thinking continues to neglect the emotional elements in economic action. These forces are neglected by the professional economist because he cannot understand them on the scientific level without making a serious study of psychology. In fact, to fully understand them, the economist would himself have to submit to psychoanalysis. An economist could not understand the emotional or psychological elements of economics only by studying other people. An intimate knowledge of psychology can be gained only by using oneself as a laboratory of experience, and the study would have to be conducted under trained guidance.

Whenever an industry gives people an increased feeling of richness, it will be successful. This will be true whether a business produces amazingly good values at very low cost, as the variety chains did, or amazingly good values at a very high monetary figure, as the television industry did.

So far I have mentioned only those industries whose sales are controlled by the psychological or non-psychological demands of consumers. Some very important industries are controlled by the demands of businessmen. These men are supposed to be strictly unemotional, but of course this is merely what they try to be. What they are is men. With a man the richness of living is felt very intensely through his mind. This is because his body is not creative. During moments when a woman is lovingly playing with his body she is trying to show him how important the body is and a man may feel this so long as he can abandon himself to her. But then he cannot abandon himself forever because his body cannot create, it can just convey; but with his mind he can create and so he goes back to thinking. Their constant thinking over the centuries has placed men in a great position compared with the one they started from, and it is for this reason that they place a great value on reason—so great a value that they often forget that they are actually still creatures of nature rather than of reason. Businessmen unwittingly often use reason to excuse their passions. Business decisions, like many typical consumer decisions, are not made on the basis of logic but on the basis of a desire for some type of richness of experience.

One such richness of experience is, of course, profit—the logical objective of a business enterprise—and there is always some correspondence between this logical objective and the richness of experience desired by the officers of the business. But the relationship is not continuous or precise. Many business decisions are excused on the basis of profit without profit being the real explanation for them. When the profit fails to materialize, the executives search around for further excuses. They themselves are very seldom entirely aware that they invested the corporation's money to gain some sort of pleasure for themselves, and that there never was any chance that their decision might be profitable—it could only be pleasurable.

It is interesting to look at the dividend records of some important companies and compare these with their records of investment in new facilities. You'll quite often reach the conclusion that the additional investment did not pay off for the stockholders. There are all sorts of rationalizations for this—or even good reasons. A management will say that it had to modernize to meet competition, or that it had to invest in research because progress is the life of business— "you either go forward or you go backward" is one of the favorite expressions of corporate management. This is true, but there are many ways of going forward or backward; it is not totally a question of will. Every businessman or group of managers is caught up in a vortex of the total world-wide desire not only to be alive but feel alive. Every businessman sooner or later finds himself in a position which he cannot control and discovers that from the profit point of view a great deal of what he had done was useless. But I doubt that many of them wish they hadn't done it and had the money. They spent the money on pleasure—a much more subtle pleasure than such a personal one as taking a luxurious vacation, or being involved with an extravagant woman or taking an adult education course in some aspect of culture. Because it is not called a pleasure, the business-men involved are free to spend much larger sums than they ever could on those things which are called pleasures and act with much greater magnificence and force.

I came back to New York once in a corporate airplane. It was one of the newest and fastest planes, costing, with all its elegant bar and galley, $1,000,000. If you figured its seating capacity and estimated the miles it might travel, you couldn't really justify it as an investment. The research director of the company said, "I wish I had had that million for something else." The head of the company had the same sort of respect for research that he had for going to church on Sunday. He wouldn't think of not doing either, but he really loved display and ostentation. He never handed out a single cigar to a visitor; instead he leaned back toward his humidor and rolled out half a dozen across the desk. So the $1,000,000 spent on the new turbo-prop made him feel big. It probably didn't help him put over any deals. His main customers were people like General Motors or Ford or General Electric and they had even more expensive private planes and also more of them. He still felt little in comparison with them but he felt he belonged to this club of the high and the mighty, whereas if he had retained the DC-3 his profits might have been bigger but he wouldn't have felt so high and mighty.

The grandiosity of the feeling for richness is a main source of practical economic richness. This desire to feel one's aliveness to the maximum is something all people have. If we really did have the DC-3 psychology, people as a whole would be much poorer than they are. This man did not understand research very well, but he did understand luxury and was considered one of the greatest executives in his industry, and Wall Street had great faith in him.

It would have been better still if he had understood the grandeur of research. I used to urge him to spend 5 per cent of his annual cash flow in discovering new industries: "For what you pay for a flying shear you could start an electronics company. You sometimes buy a piece of equipment that doesn't work too well—what's worse about losing money that way than in getting experience in a new business?" He nodded his head pleasantly. My reasoning was good. If he had taken my advice when I gave it, the market value of his stock could easily have turned out to be double or triple what it was. And, of course, if he had really understood this, it would have satisfied his feeling for grandeur and he would have done it. What he understood was where grandeur lay for him.

CHAPTER TWO

The Exuberant Force of Non-Reason

One of the important reasons why stocks go up and down is for "non-reasons" rather than reasons. You may think this is a whimsical statement but you should reflect that science acknowledges the value of the negative as well as the positive. Non-scientific people, which means most of us most of the time, don't have a passionate interest in negatives. And it's still true that being non-scientific can be very effective.

The Romans, for instance, were extremely successful people, though perhaps it isn't quite fair to call them non-scientific since they were great engineers. But they were not the theoretical sort of scientific people. Mathematics and astronomy slipped backward from the Greeks and their empire ended in an unscientific Christian mess, waiting for the second coming of Christ.

It was the Arabs who first understood the power of the negative—of zero and the minus numbers which go to the left of zero. Arab civilization ended in a mess too. They probably would have done just as well or badly if they had not discovered the zero—a state which doesn't exist in the world of human sensation but does exist in the world of thought which is also a real world. And the world of the senses is, unfortunately for the thinkers, a real world too. The trouble with Wendell Willkie was that he wanted to make it "One World." It always sounds good and everybody is always trying to make it one world—namely, theirs. But there happens to be, always under any condition, at least two worlds, yours and an opposite.

Well, just to clinch the case, physicists have recently discovered anti-matter. Apparently it exists in outer space. Outer space is big and so anti-matter and matter don't often meet. But when they do, each is annihilated. Since the annihilation of matter creates energy, this meeting of the positive and negative proves the value of each—the existence of one heightens the possibilities of the other.

As a stock goes up, someone calls up and asks, "Why?" The phone in my office rings, a voice says, "I suppose you know that Kay Kemical has been active and strong, four thousand shares traded, which is a lot for that stock and it's up three points. You know what the story is? It's going to split two for one after the close and they'll declare a 4-percent dividend."

So I try to get Joe, Kay Kemical's president. Joe's "in a meeting," so I guess there is something to the story. I check with the specialist in the stock on the floor of the exchange. "All I expect is a 3-per-cent stock dividend."

Late that afternoon Joe calls me.

"What did you do?"

"We declared a 3-per-cent stock dividend."

"The rumor was," I told him, "that you would split it two for one, declare 4 per cent as a dividend."

This was all news to Joe but it was what made the stock go up. The truth would have had some effect but fiction had more. Who started the fiction?

When I was talking to Joe, he had said, "Hamburger and Company called up and asked if it were true about a stock split and I said no."

"Gee, Joe," I said. "My man said that Hamburger is the

one who told him there would be a split and also a 4-per-cent dividend."

Who started the rumor? No one ever knows. It's just a non-fact creating a fact in the market: the rise or fall of some stock.

Rumors like this are very common—perhaps you would call them reasons rather than non-reasons. The distinction is, however, worthwhile. Stocks go up for reasons which are non-factual as well as for those which are factual. Both are extremely effective in putting stocks up or down but people who live in the factual world are always going to have a hard time understanding why this is so. The reason is simple—there are two worlds to which stocks respond, the non-factual as well as the factual.

The powers of non-reason are, of course, why stocks can be promoted so effectively. If investors were not responsive to the forces of non-reason, if they had to be sure of the facts before they acted, stocks could not be promoted. The regulatory authorities are all on the side of reason—investigate before you invest, they cry. Whenever a company sells new shares to the public or whenever controlling insiders—officers, directors, or stockholders—sell more than a certain modest amount of their holdings, the shares have to be registered and a prospectus has to be issued by the company under the supervision of the Securities and Exchange Commission; everything in the prospectus sticks to the facts. It makes extremely dull reading.

Some years ago each prospectus was voluminously buttressed with facts. They were expensive to prepare and few ever read them. Now investors are issued a short form of the basic prospectus. It would be a mistake to say that the information in the prospectus, limited as it is, is never the reason why investors buy stocks. For one thing, facts sometimes can be choreographed even though the S.E.C. is watching.

I remember when a very prominent drug company did some financing after World War II. It was in the late spring and the company's report for the first quarter of the year was out. When the prospectus came out later, it showed the sales and earnings for the first four months. By subtracting the report of the first three months from the four months' report shown in the prospectus, investors were able to see what had happened in April, the most recent month. The good results were amazing.

This was during the first antibiotic boom. The company was the leader in antibiotics and had recently put a new one on the market. Investors, especially the studious type given to close study of prospectuses, when they saw what happened in April, jumped to the conclusion that the business was in orbit. If you multiplied the earnings of April by 12, you got a much bigger projection of full year's earnings than if you multiplied the results of the first quarter by 4.

This isn't considered sound statistics but it was sound financing. The stock skyrocketed and the underwriting was a huge success. The earnings for the year did not, in the end, turn out to be as good as the April results indicated they might, so the stock was lower at the end of the year.

Since then, everything has turned out for the best—no permanent harm was really done. It was just a maneuver designed to get a better price for the stock at the time of the financing.

How was it done? I really don't know. I merely suspect. It may have been an accident that April was so good, one of those lucky things that sometimes happens to companies and people. It's sort of an axiom in sports that winners are lucky. But I think it could have been done this way: the management could have stimulated sales during April in various ways. They could simply have asked their better-natured customers to take delivery by April 30 of what would normally be shipped early in May. They could also have held back deliveries of low-profit items, pushed the high-profit ones. These efforts would have produced both a rise in total sales and a spectacular jump in profit margin. The company could have followed its usual accounting procedures and the S.E.C. would never have known what really happened.

I remember once, while I was flying from San Francisco to Salt Lake City, reading a prospectus of a uranium stock I had bought. I often feel nervous in planes even on a beautiful calm day. I looked out the window of the DC-6 and saw the mountains below and after them, the Great Salt Desert. It didn't look like the best terrain on which to land, so I thought I would read about some of the sober aspects of the company in which I had invested.

When I read the bare facts, all my fear of flying disappeared. Fear of what would happen to my dollars took its place. I didn't have to worry though; most speculators were doing the same thing I had done—buying first, reading later. The stock tripled.

Actually, the facts outlined in the prospectus didn't tell the full story. They couldn't tell for example the psychological resourcefulness and force of this company's management. Having traveled around the uranium company with its president, I had a different feeling about the company than any factual review of its short history could convey. In this case, the feeling had more validity than the facts in the prospectus.

Uncertain facts are not bad; the only thing is, you can't be sure they are facts. But the certainty of facts can be deceiving, as I mentioned in the case of the pharmaceutical company. Stocks can be promoted in two ways—by the willful planting of fiction and by the willful planting of certain but misleading facts. All the truth and nothing but the truth is not the same as all the facts and nothing but the facts. Things which aren't facts can be a true guide.

Because facts can be deceiving, the non-reasons which move stocks are not always invalid. Non-reasons and reasons can each be deceptive or valid. However, since non-reasons are relatively non-factual, they are the favorite force of promoters. For instance, one day International Telephone and Raytheon were both active and strong on the tape. A friend of mine called saying, "Did you hear anything about a merger of International and Raytheon?" I happened to have very good contacts with International Telephone through its president, Harold Geneen, and his brilliant assistant, David Margolies. When Harold, years ago, was comptroller of Jones and Laughlin, a major producer of steel, we used to have many talks about how foolish the steel industry was not to invest some minor percentage of its huge income in new industries. This common feeling we had that the steel industry was using its resources unimaginatively made Harold and me close friends.

When Raytheon offered him a job as executive vice president, he jumped. He did wonders for Raytheon, and then International Telephone asked him to become their president, so he moved again. When the rumor about a merger of Raytheon and I.T. popped, I knew he or Dave would give me some idea as to the facts.

Dave said, "That must have been one of the best-distributed rumors ever. I've heard from every corner of the United States in the last half hour." There was absolutely nothing in it. Someone apparently wanted to move one of the stocks, maybe both. But probably, just one. And a well-organized rumor was initiated. This goes on all the time but sometimes the rumors are true.

A West Coast newspaper sent me this telegram, "Hear Stuffy Chemical will acquire Ozone Chemical Works. Can you check?"

Ozone Chemical was then selling for about half what Stuffy was. On checking, I wasn't able to get a yes-or-no response. A few weeks later I got a much better indication that the rumor probably was correct. One of the officers of one of the companies had been buying Ozone for his relatives. His customer's man chatted to a friend of mine and, for some reason, he was candid enough to talk to me in detail when I phoned him. This wasn't absolutely sure confirmation but it was very close and quite profitable.

At some point in every boom a situation is being created wherein investors are getting ready to take a loss, although they don't know it. This point is impossible to know in advance. A boom does not exist for no reason at all. The reasons behind it are not false. A boom represents an exaggeration of truth, not a lack of truth. The force that leads to exaggeration is that of non-reason, not the force of no reason at all. There is a difference between non-reason and no reason. Non-reason, in terms of force, is positive, just as a minus number in terms of mathematical power has force or just as anti-matter in terms of mass has the potency of becoming energy and, perhaps, other potencies besides that. Non-reason is the opposite of reason; it is not a non-existing thing.

Non-reason obviously deals with that part of future development which cannot be described with reason. We know there is a potential, but we do not know exactly what it is and we cannot know. In the stock market we describe this potential on the ticker tape. As our conviction about it increases, the prices go up. Part of this potential may be described by things we know or at least we think we know. For instance, we all agree that the computer industry is in for very rapid growth in the next decade; estimates have been made as to how huge this business will become. Some of these estimates have been made privately by companies which sell components to computer manufacturers or by the computer manufacturers themselves.

Other estimates are publicly available, estimates such as those made by *Fortune* magazine. These estimates become part of the known facts of the industry. The estimates themselves may prove wrong but, for the moment, they serve as guides to our thinking about the industry. If you are interested in a computer manufacturing company, you may ask your broker, "How big will this industry get?" He doesn't know, no one knows for sure, it's still a very young industry. He may say, "*Fortune* magazine has made a careful survey—this will give you some idea."

Then you take this estimate of *Fortune*'s and try to figure out how much I.B.M. might make in 1965 if the survey proves reasonably accurate and if I.B.M. gets a certain share of the business—maybe 50 per cent, maybe 75 per cent. You play around with the possibilities and you arrive at an estimate which is more definite than you would have if no one had made a survey of the future possible sales of computers. This definiteness may be misleading, of course, but at least it is based on reason. Or you could just buy I.B.M. because you had a big, big feeling about computers.

This big, big feeling would represent non-reason; the estimate of *Fortune* would represent reason. Since no one can tell how big the business may really get, his estimate doesn't represent truth, just reason. The trouble with reason is its definiteness. It looks like truth, or at least we always expect truth to be something we can know or prove, but this definiteness of reason can be a lie and the big, big feeling can be nearer to the truth.

What an investor is always looking for is some type of insight. You have to accept the sort of insight you have and not be concerned with what you lack. It's obvious that a person who doesn't give a damn about balancing his checkbook is never going to have much insight into the office machine industry.

To get back to reason and non-reason—the non-reason force which has made computers a great growth industry is people and especially man's insatiable desire to feel sure of himself. Being up-to-date means being sure of where you are. This may or may not lead to a more intelligent decision as to what the next step should be. Theoretically it should lead to a more intelligent decision. Certainly one cannot argue that being out-of-date is the best thing to be. In that case we would have to construct non-computers, machines which scrambled everything up so the executive would have use for his imagination and start over again. Actually this might be a very good machine to have, but we are not going to build them.

This insatiable desire to know, or think we know, is why we have newspapers, radio, television, telephones, and now the rapidly growing data-processing industry. Now that we have these things, we can't go back to the quill pen or the pony express, even though history shows that some very great thoughts were thought and things done in those times. I am not one of those people who think we should go back to the compost heap for our garden fertilizer or the water-driven millstone for grinding our grains. I tried some of this mill-stoned flour once in homemade bread and I saw instantly why white flour became so popular once the commercial mills knew how to make it.

It isn't a question of what do we like or whether we think it's good or bad. It's a question of what is, and one of the big forces driving us on is uncertainty. Therefore anything which makes us feel more certain is something we will spend money on. There are other forces making computers a big industry, other reasons than this non-reason force and very likely other non-reason forces. Computers are essential for I.C.B.M.'s or for space-probing rockets. Without a computer keeping track of where they were going, they wouldn't know what to do. So a reasonable reason for the growth of the computer industry is that we will need vast amounts of tele-metering equipment. That sounds very reasonable and sensible, but then the question is, why do we need rockets?

Again one of the non-reasons making us spend billions on rockets is this question of uncertainty. The questions of who we are, what is life, where are we going are the biggest of all questions for men and a big one certainly for women, though women don't seem to care too much who they are so long as they are married. But a man is different. There is no way that he gets that certainty out of his existence itself. He can only get that certainty through a final knowledge of the big existence which he thinks must exist.

Since non-reason deals with mystery, whereas reason deals with what we think we understand enough to describe, there is a tendency at times to feel that those who are attuned to non-reason are somehow wiser than those who are attuned to reason. In a certain way this is true. Most people feel that human progress depends on gradually reducing all things to reason and that non-reason represents the irrational, the illogical, the undesirable. But primarily this isn't true. Non-reason represents mystery, the thing that we don't know. Obviously this much be much larger than what we do know. The reasonable people feel that we are going to know more and more—like walking down a road and coming around a bend. This is true in a sense but it doesn't mean that mystery necessarily gets less and less—mystery may be expanding. The non-reasonable people feel that they have some sort of insight into this mystery which makes them more profound than the reasonable people. This is true in cases where reasonable people ignore mystery or regard it as an unopened case and plod along as though the non-opening of the case kept the mystery effectively in a package. But mystery is an operative thing—and this feeling of the operativeness of mystery does give non-reasonable people a certain type of profundity which reasonable people lack. But the non-reasonable people inevitably make a cult of mystery, thinking they know something about it which they don't. What they do have is a respect for mystery. When they think they know something about it, they begin to be reasonable in a cockeyed way. The non-reasonable people push stocks to rather cockeyed prices at times but the reasonable people keep on missing something that is there because they can't understand it. The unusually gifted speculator or investor, like the unusually gifted artist, is a person who really can't be explained. He has some sort of understanding of where to be non-reasonable and where to become reasonable. Translated into the market, he has a sort of feeling for not taking profits too soon and then suddenly taking them.

The force of non-reason, great as it is, has its limits. At some point all booms end. Both reason and non-reason have their limits. Perhaps, together, they are unlimited; I don't know. Perhaps, just as the collision of matter and anti-matter represents annihilation, so a combination of reason and non-reason represents something without limit, but they never have been in combination and there always have been limits.

If you accept the duality of the situation, you will understand the market. Sometimes you will be able to benefit from your understanding and at others you will simply enjoy your understanding. Stocks move up and down for both reasons and non-reasons. Sometimes their movements are due to clear, logical, adequate reasons and at other times they seem to contradict all logic and good sense. Sometimes the good sense develops later and you begin to see that there was a type of reason behind the movement which at one time you did not understand. Sometimes the good sense does not develop. The force of non-reason ends and stocks go down.

CHAPTER THREE

The Speed of Wealth Can Mean
Wealth Without Effort

If you have seen many great fortunes built during your lifetime, you naturally have a different feeling about them than if you merely had read of them. The time we live in is a great one for fortune building and my position in Wall Street has been a good one from which to see it happen. There are more fortunes both great and little than ever before because the world is far wealthier than it has ever been and in the future the multiplicity of fortunes will be greater still. The day may come when the world's productivity is such that everyone has at least a small fortune. This is not a statistical impossibility though it also is not a geological or an agricultural certainty.

The table below shows you the fortunes which have been made recently and indicates the speed with which they have actually been made. The table is made up of simple facts given in the prospectuses of a number of companies which sold stock to the public between 1955 and 1960. It is far from being, or intended to be, conclusive. But it shows what has been done and therefore what can be done—in fact what is bound to be done so long as private enterprise lasts, no matter what taxes or other restraints are levied. If wealth is created, someone is going to get it, and in a capitalist country some of the bright and/or lucky ones are going to get a lot of it.

Table I.

SOME FORTUNES CREATED 1955–59
BY SALE OF INTERESTS IN PRIVATELY HELD COMPANIES TO PUBLIC

	Shares Owned by Principal Owner	Principal Owner's Share Equity Prior to Offering	Value at Offering Price	Value at Current Market	%Shares Owned by Principal	
					Before Offering	After Offering
Dashew	755,462 [1]	$596,594	$10,387,603	$18,886,550	75.5%	65.7%
Biochemical	78,159 [2]	88,200	586,192	1,094,226	48.8	30.1
Owens Yacht	175,000 [3]	798,151	2,000,000	2,525,000	25.0	17.5
Tool Research	142,542 [4]	197,000	570,168	2,138,130	47.5	25.9
FXR Corp.	111,500 [5]	544,311	1,938,100	3,833,500	50.0	25.8

[1] Stanley A. Dashew.
[2] S. Louis Gaines.
[3] Charles J. Owen—250,000 shrs prior; 75,000 sold.
[4] Leopold S. Wyler, Jr.
[5] Henry Feldman—161,500 shrs prior; 50,000 sold.

If science can develop enough effective ways to use the resources of the universe, including of course the resources of space, it would be possible for industry to outstrip the growth of population and create a fortune for everybody. On the other hand, scientific developments depend on reality. We are using up certain of our resources very rapidly, for instance, our oil, natural gas, and low-cost coal. We may unknowingly be living in a golden age of fortune which is a prelude to a decline or we may more knowingly be living in an early stage of final economic development and conquest.

To the observer the interesting characteristic of fortune building is the speed with which it can be and usually is accomplished. (*See* Table I.) Making a fortune is not particularly difficult providing you have a gift for it and providing the circumstances exist which permit you to exercise that gift.

Who, for example, would have thought 20 years ago that a talent for mathematics was a gift which might lead to a quick fortune? But as mathematics became integrated with electronics, it became a peculiarly rich gift from the economic as well as from the intellectual point of view. For example, the development of computers and their utilization in industry and in military and scientific products created an outlet for mathematic gifts which has led to hundreds of new personal fortunes.

As I have said, seeing it happen is more convincing and exciting than reading about it. I sat with a cluster of slender, febrile young men in 1953 in an Italian table d'hôte restaurant and listened to them talk about traveling mus or whatever the mathematical sign was that apparently skipped from here to there. I never thought that by 1955 they would be opening a new research center and by 1960 would be millionaires.

I liked this sort of meeting. One of them was dressed in a T-shirt, the Adam's apple of his long neck bobbing up and down as he swallowed the celery, which came free with the meal; another with a pushed-up cranium which made his forehead, under the crew cut, look low even though it was high. Wildness is always the thing that is exciting—after all, it's quite mathematical. If you are tame, it means the forces have been brought in balance or under control. And unless you can see in the balance something precarious which may lead to an unbalancing, tameness is bound to be dull, though healthy possibly. In 1953 they were free and wild. In 1955 they were still wild, but in 1960 they were rich and, naturally, not so wild. They had heavy things to hold up now and no one wanted them to fall.

Wealth really is wildness organized so that it goes like a millstream into a bank account. And that's the pity of it; only a few great geniuses like Byron or Alexander the Great or Toulouse-Lautrec or William Burroughs have been wealthy and wild—you know—in a big way.

A more common and long-standing example of gifts on which new fortunes have been built is the gift of gab. Radio and television have opened up markets for the ability to talk smoothly which didn't exist formerly. Salesmanship, of course, has always paid off, but it's not quite the same thing. The clear, resonant, well-cultivated voice is much more valuable today than the traditional trickery of salesmanship. Personality itself is what has created immense fortunes for disc jockeys. The payola helped, but payola without personality is nothing.

Because of this, people high in the entertainment world have been learning the tricks of ordinary industry and, to an increasing degree, are becoming high in the conventional business world. None of them—Ed Sullivan, Bing Crosby, Art Linkletter, Milton Berle, Faye Emerson—is remarkably old nor have they had a remarkably hard struggle. The opportunity existed and they had the gifts as well as the general aggressive ability to exploit it. Some of them might have done as well some other place or time; Bing Crosby, for example, might have been a successful railroad magnate in the nineteenth century; still, what would he have done with his voice—sing "The Public Be Damned"? The time spirit which made a Vanderbilt great might, a hundred years ago, have left Bing yodeling in some country chorus.

The complex relationship of opportunity to gift is not confined to people but exists in things too. It's amazing sometimes to see industrial opportunities open up. You look for some definite reason, for some important new revelation, and you don't find it because what is causing the new industrial opportunity is not new knowledge but a new combination of existing knowledges. Just as there have always been people who can chat amusingly, so there are elements, compounds, or applications of energy which have always had potential usefulness but only recently an outlet.

Some opportunities are opened up by sudden discovery. Uranium is the most outstanding example of a great industry born in very recent years out of sudden discovery. And the birth of this industry meant also the creation of many fortunes. But during these same years germanium, silicon, selenium, tantalum, columbium, beryllium, lithium, zirconium, and titanium have become industrially important, have created fortunes, and in some cases it is hard to assign a precise and sudden reason for the importance.

Selenium and silicon rectifiers, for example, have an interesting future because of the growing domestication of the automobile. When we raised our windows by hand, when we shoved our driver's seat back or wriggled it forward by the uncomfortable force of our muscles, when we eased the summer heat by the hot breeze of an open window, the conventional electrical system for automobiles was satisfactory. But with electrically moved windows and seats, with push-button gear shifts and with air-conditioning, the electrical system of automobiles will have to be made more and more elaborate and this will mean a market for the materials and techniques which go into them, such as selenium and silicon.

The most startling of new wealth developments have been the various ways which have been found to use the electron more efficiently. Unknown to most people, the electron is the heart of the chemical industry. This is because when two elements unite to make a compound, the bond is made between their orbital electrons. The protons and neutrons forming the nuclei of the elements do not merge into a new nucleus. If they did, this would be atomic fusion, and it is possible that, in the future, controlled atomic fusion will be a big new business using tremendous quantities of various materials and producing tremendous amounts of power as well as certain elements or compounds—but for the present the only marketable product of atomic fusion is the hydrogen bomb and efforts are being made to limit this. At any rate, the now familiar synthetic chemical products would never have existed unless improved ways had been found to manipulate electrons. The huge, familiar electric power industry also represents a past discovery in the handling of electrons in wires. Discoveries of this sort made Edison and others suddenly rich. More recently than that, discovery of ways to control the flow of electrons in vacuum tubes built the huge radio and television networks, and in very recent years ways have been found to control the flow of electrons in very small pieces of material—germanium, silicon, gallium arsenide. This is called solid state physics, and in the last three or four years huge stock market fortunes have been created for the major owners of Transitron, Fairchild Camera, Texas Instruments, Varian Associates, etc.

But part of these fortunes were made by public excitement about these discoveries rather than the discoveries themselves. Investors were willing to pay more for the mystery of the new thing than the proven values of the old. This is always going to be the case. Mystery has a tremendous value; proved values have—well, you know what they are and that's what they have—but mystery is something you don't know. During 1961 the stock of International Business Machines was given a total value of over $11,000,000,000 by the market. This was substantially more than double the market value of the stocks of all the 20 railroads included in the Dow Jones Railroad Stock Average. It's true that railroading is a declining industry. Still these companies, in some cases, had enormous assets in oil, uranium, city real estate, timber lands, etc., as well as rail mileage, and the rail mileage had many years of usefulness left in it—but these are familiar rather than mysterious values. I.B.M. stood for computers, input and output equipment, memory storage—lots of things which most of us are only beginning to vaguely understand the usefulness of. When computers are as familiar as cash registers, I.B.M. will sell at a much less romantic value—you wait and see.

There is a particular moment when the value of mystery is at its greatest. When most investors are completely ignorant, they don't pay much for mystery—many of these stocks could have been bought at very reasonable prices in 1957. There is a special moment when everyone sees that something amazing is coming out of mystery and then they will pay a lot more to know more about this strange new thing. Later on, when mystery has given birth, when they know more, they will pay less. Thus most of the electronic stocks which boomed in 1959–61 will be selling for less in 1965, and all of them, I feel sure, will be selling for less in relation to their earnings. In other words, those companies which fulfill the vision of 1959 will be much better known to investors by 1965, and their stocks will be given a rating of knowledge rather than of mystery.

For most of us our greatest richness always has been and still remains in dreams. It may be in dreams about our future accomplishments, it may be in dreams about how wonderful it would be to meet that girl on the diving raft, it may be in dreams of our children, or dreams of the past recalled, or of revenge and future justice, or of religion and another world. We cannot hope for economic riches which are really greater than our dreams, but it is also true that economic riches can help our dreams. A beautiful home makes a woman dream more, she can be marvelously content.

Because no wealth you will ever have—even if you are the richest man in the world—will equal your dreams, stocks go to particularly high levels when a lot of people think they might equal their dreams. Those stocks which are called growth stocks might better be called dream stocks. But dreams are real—we have them every day. It's a big mistake to think that dreams are unreal and what is called real life is real. If dreams were unreal, it would be possible for you to feel richer than your dreams if you were the richest man in the world. When the dream of a new industry comes true, then the dream ends and the stocks sell more conservatively, relating to what is real rather than to what was dreamed.

One of the astonishing economic developments of our times and one of the greatest of the fortune-building forces has been the move to the suburbs. This has been created by many developments, the most important of these being the unexpected, inexplicable psychology of human beings. Years ago people commuted too, but the distances were short. Thirty minutes on the train was considered drastic.

During the war I spent two hours trainfaring each way. There were six or seven of us in a little Connecticut town who did it and we were considered slightly insane. Now thousands of people commute from this town. The unexpected willingness of men to live from one-twelfth to one-sixth of their adult lives in a state of travel has radically altered the value of country real estate and created fortunes for those who have a feeling for that business.

From seeing how rapidly fortunes are made, and this observation can be buttressed by endless references to history, it is very important to realize that if money making doesn't come easy, it means there is something wrong. This

something may mean that you yourself aren't really interested in making money—you just think you are, or that you
live in the wrong place or are in the wrong occupation—or
it may simply mean that the time isn't ripe for what you do.
As I pointed out previously, if you were a mathematician in
1920 (or a nuclear physicist, or even an electronics engineer)
—and these occupations represented your real love, outside of
your wife—you were very unlikely to be able to make a fortune no matter how hard you tried. You might, if you had
been that sort of person at that time, have given up and tried
something else—and if you could have been happy doing
something else that could have been a wise choice, but if
you had been this sort of person working between 1950 and
1960 you could scarcely have avoided wealth; certainly if you
were any good at all, you could not have avoided a good
salary. Making money, as I have said, is partly a question of
time and place and partly that of personal skill and effort.
When you do make money you are bound to make it fast—it
won't come slowly, for in that case it won't come at all.

When I say something like this, people think I am cynical.
Maybe they think it's clever, maybe they think it's cheap—
but they don't think it's real. The facts, however, show it is
real. Wealth, when it came at all, has always come quickly
and easily. You can read up on all the old fortunes; you can
go back to the days of Julius Caesar, when wealth was made
in a battle; check up on Rockefeller, Carnegie, Ford—anyone
you want; and you will find that most people who start out
poor and end up rich do it while they are still young. There
may be years of struggle before they hit it, and maybe they
had to keep on struggling in order to be there when the opportunity came, but when the opportunity came, it was like
the dawn breaking—when the sun rises, it moves up quickly.

I have made a lot of money quickly and also worked hard

on things which never paid off. This book had been written and rewritten over a period of years. But the thing is, I made money in other ways. The most and easiest money I ever made was from $500 I put into the Vitramon Corporation. This was just an accident. Barton Weller, a young electrical engineer employed by a subsidiary of Du Pont, lived near by. He had interested a Wall Street broker, who also lived in the area of those Connecticut hills, in putting money into a company which would try to perfect, manufacture, and sell a type of electrical component which Du Pont scientists had invented during World War II. Weller had researched the market for Du Pont and decided there was a market waiting for the capacitor. Du Pont decided there wasn't, so Weller left and raised $25,000 in the neighborhood. Chick Sartorious put in most; a scientist specializing in ceramics, which was an essential part of the new device, put in the next largest amount; Herbert Simonds, a world-famed expert on plastics, put in some; and since I knew Herbert well and was also from Wall Street, I put in a bit and went on the Board of Directors. I didn't know at the time what a capacitor was, let alone why ours (which was very expensive) should be what anybody wanted—I just went along for the ride. My chief virtue on the Board was that I would talk loudly, lengthily, and frankly, and then vote yes—if that was the vote they wanted. The company had a horrible time. Du Pont was absolutely right. We were broke and bankrupt at least once a year. One year some solvent got on Bart, ignited, and sent him to the hospital for six months. The company was still housed in his basement. The doors were closed and I wrote off my $500 in my income-tax report. When Bart got out of bed he found a small vacant building, and we were in business again on a much larger scale. I had to correct my tax report. We began to make some money and we hired a ceramics expert to improve our yields. The yields completely collapsed. We were broke again. I think it was at this meeting that I suggested to our secretary—Dorothy Kasparait, who had an endless woman's faith in Bart and the business, and who became a very rich woman later because of this faith—that she count the postage stamps to see what our total liquid assets were. I think I made my one valuable contribution to the progress of the firm at this meeting by pointing out that we might have low yields for a very long time, and that we would have to raise our prices to make some money on what we could get out of the process. Bart took my advice and we lost our biggest customer. This was lucky, because we were losing money on everything we shipped him. We began to make a little money on our remaining smaller customers, who were principally people holding defense contracts for some experimental work. By 1956 we were finally making some real money and Bart gave a Christmas party for employees and stockholders. After that the Pentagon went into one of its economy drives, and by the middle of 1957 we were not far from broke again. During these years I had bought some more stock when it was offered at a few dollars. We were rescued from the 1957 slump by Sputnik and the accelerated building of missiles. Finally, in 1960, we were big and prosperous enough to offer stock to the public. The public was willing to give our stock an initial value on the first trading day of over nine million dollars. Bart, who owned 51 per cent of the company, had about five million dollars in marketable securities. My original $500 was worth almost $50,000. Now it's true that Bart Weller worked extremely hard, with what might be called true dogged courage; in other words, a reasonable person would have quit many years ago. But I didn't work at all. I attended the Directors' meetings faithfully because I liked the people there.

We had coffee and doughnuts and it was a pleasant way to pass some time. I never really understood the company—I couldn't honestly say that I saw in Bart a great genius because I honestly didn't. There were other members of the Board who understood him this way. I really saw his weaknesses more clearly. I am saying this not to give you a true confession but to emphasize a true experience—that of making a very substantial amount of money with no real effort, with a minimum of foresight—just by what I believe can truly be called luck, and also to emphasize that there has to be a right opportunity for it. Missiles gave Vitramon its great opportunity; Bart's dogged courage and scientific perception made the company ready for it; I had a picnic.

Fortune-making, when it is not an expression of luck, is an art. There is a great deal about it which cannot be explained, at least not in the simple, rational way in which people like things to be explained, but like art, it must absorb your interest intensely. People who make fortunes are either intensely interested in their occupation which accidentally brings them a fortune, or they are intensely interested in money, or they have some combination of these intensities.

Picasso, Matisse, de Kooning, for instance, made fortunes out of painting. There are many wealthy artists today. Because of the financial success of artists, the art school business is booming. It is unlikely, however, that among the hundreds of thousands of men and women who take courses that there will be many Picassos. Some of the schools will probably never have a distinguished student, even though the vast majority of their students are undoubtedly gifted. Added to such gifts must be an intense excitement with the activity of being an artist. It must be beyond the call of reason and therefore beyond the test of money. Wealth will eventually come out of the occupation as a by-product.

Obviously the inability of art schools to teach people how to be artistic geniuses is matched by the inability of any book or course of education on Wall Street to teach you how to be a financial genius. This is the truth—sad or otherwise—which, if you don't believe now, you'll agree with later.

But a school can give you a point of view. The difference between a good art teacher and a poor one is not so much the specific things they teach, for these—such as how to mix paints—are rather limited; the difference is the point of view. A school can give you a start, it can give you technical hints, and if it has the right point of view (and if you have the excitement), you can go a long way. Would Picasso have been Picasso if he had been a young man in America? Probably not. No young American painter of his time became internationally important, though certainly many were gifted and had excitement in their art. Would be have become a great artist if he had been a young man in America 20 years later? The chances would have been better. What if he had been a young man starting to paint 30 years later? He would almost certainly have been one of the world's great artists. Art in America had by then gotten on the right road—it had moved away from the limited concepts and provincialism which held it back. How did this happen? Not through any one book or any one school. It was a complex development. The real thing you hope for in any type of education which is involved with questions of art rather than science is some sort of push in the right direction. This must be in the direction of reality. But what is reality? True reality is the search of every artist. The push is not toward the discovery but toward the search.

The reason that wealth can be made so swiftly is because of the relationship of time and intelligence.

It is time that has accumulated the materials from which

intelligence can produce wealth. Time has accumulated the petroleum, the coal, the various ores of the earth. It has molded the continents, the river basins, the mountain ranges; it has established the various climates in the locations they now are; it has allowed the sea to store up its minerals.

To a certain extent, the possibilities of anything are related to the time needed to produce it. We can think of the making of earth or the universe the way we think of any productive process. It is related to time. It took a certain number of years to make the earth, perhaps some billions before it became as it now is.

It is obvious that something which took several billion years to come into being has an immense potential if all, or a large part, of what has been created in this time can be used.

The billions of years needed to create the earth therefore has a practical significance to businessmen. It is not just an academic fact which will never affect the computer. The stupendous history of the earth and of the universe is business's biggest, though possibly most hidden, asset.

A billion years is even less conceivable to the average human being than a billion dollars. No one has ever had any direct contact with a billion years. The inconceivable immensity of time can be thought of as forecasting the inconceivable immensity of future opportunity. If the intelligence can dig out of the storehouse of time a really large percentage of the material which has been accumulated, and put it into useful forms, then the human race, by this interaction of time and intelligence, can become immensely wealthy.

An important factor in this situation is that time is inherently slow while intelligence is inherently fast. Intelligence frequently works by a process that develops an idea instantaneously. "It came to me in a flash." Sometimes a considerable body of experience has to precede the flash of inspiration, but it is important to reflect that the key idea which unlocks the solution to a problem often comes quickly.

Flight by man, for example, is not new as an idea, but it is recent as a fact. The change from poetic fantasy to business fact did not develop gradually year by year. It lay dormant in impracticalities for centuries and then, when it became practical, the change from fantasy to fact was blinding in its speed.

Petroleum is something Noah knew about but petroleum wasn't cracked until 1848. So if we want to, we can trace the origin of flight back a century. The invention of efficient gasoline engines was the most important single factor making airplanes possible. Before we could have the engine, we had to have gasoline. Still, a century isn't a long time as history goes. Flight to the moon, when scientists were writing about it ten years ago, still seemed pure fantasy to most of us. We didn't realize how rapidly some of the accumulated forces of nature were being organized so we could use them.

If it were the nature of the intelligence to move slowly, then it would be virtually impossible to solve human economic problems. The creation of human wealth would be inherently the same tedious slow process used by time to store up its raw materials. It is the possibility of multiplying the mass of time by the speed of the intelligence which gives the human race the right to have high economic hopes. If all that time has stored up in a few billion years can be put to use in a few thousand, or better, in a few hundred, then the possibilities of wealth are fabulous.

It is, therefore, in the nature of things that wealth can be made very rapidly. When a person gets rich quick, it's not a fluke. It's in line with the logic of the universe; it's explainable by the relationships of time and intelligence. Therefore, of all the ways of getting rich, getting rich quick is the best.

Then it leaves you time for other things, and what you have to hope is that you have an understanding of other things.

For the human race as a whole, their only hope is that some day they will get rich quick. There is no chance for the race as a whole if they have to do it the hard way. There has been a long struggle for the race and there may be centuries of struggle ahead. But I don't think so. I think there is the possibility of very drastic and rapid general change. In that case, becoming wealthy will be less of an art and more of a natural condition. This may seem an absurd idea but, after all, it's really what has been going on. In my childhood millionaires were rare. One joined our golf club. He built what seemed to us a palace—it was made of stucco (a new material to the Midwest) and looked like a cross between the White House and an Italian castle. This was quite astounding, but the biggest thing was the swimming pool. Swimming pools in Illinois were as widely scattered as oases in Arabia. I don't have to tell you how common swimming pools are today. It's just one of many signs of how widespread real wealth has become. The problem of an investor isn't really that of making money but rather that of understanding the growth of wealth. If he understands this he has a very good chance of finding some way to derive an unusual benefit from it—and if wealth develops in practice, as it could in theory, then even the average investor in enterprise will find himself unusually fortunate. He will benefit from that strange and little-recognized force of nature—wealth without effort.

CHAPTER FOUR

Dr. Jekyll & Mr. Hyde in Economics

I was in the office of a Mr. Hyde of industry, some of whose financiers acquired their original capital from past illegal services which, as I shall describe later, turned out for the benefit of the nation. From his window he could see the back end of his open-hearth shop, the end from which the steel is poured when the furnace is tapped. Suddenly he jumped up. "Did you hear that?" he asked. "That means they're tapping a heat." We hurried to his car and drove to the open hearths. On the way he told me how his company had been the first to use Du Pont's new cartridge method of tapping a furnace. A shaped charge of explosive breaks the plug and lets the fiery steel out. It gave him a great deal of pleasure to think that his rickety little steel company had been the first to use a technical innovation while some of the great, respectable Dr. Jekylls of the industry were still letting their men hammer out the plugs with long, heavy bars.

His company was making money—lots of it. It was a case of sudden riches. A year ago it had been losing, but the steel boom which was especially strong in the products his mill made had changed the situation. This year he could get premium prices from desperate customers who could not get the steel they needed at list prices from the big companies. A year back he had had to peddle his metal under the market to get any business at all. His stock was a good buy, I thought, even if his plant was dilapidated, because he was earning enough to balance the bad features in the situation.

The next morning I had breakfast with two Dr. Jekylls of industry. You couldn't find two more respectable or more able businessmen in America. Nor could you find a much better company. In its particular chemical speciality, it was tops, its research possibly the most thorough and extensive in the field of plastic films. Except for cellophane which was pioneered by Du Pont, it has been the leader in developing plastic films. Its stock had a high investment rating because of its leadership, its record, its research, and what one would assume to be its future. But as the two Dr. Jekylls talked on, I detected a sour note. Competition was becoming tougher in one of its two major divisions. Other firms that did less research and who had borrowed from what the Dr. Jekylls' company had pioneered were turning out as good a product and were taking business away. For applications which had become well established, the major research had been completed. The smaller operators were benefiting, without saying thank you, from the research done by the larger company.

In listening to and questioning the Dr. Jekylls, I had to be tactful because of their high respectability. When Dr. Ted Jekyll softly mentioned lower profit margins on polyethylene film, I could hardly believe my ears. The conversation flowed swiftly to something else. I used care in bringing the conversation back to this topic, because I was afraid that if too much emphasis was put on it, they would begin to modify their not entirely conscious admissions.

In talking to Mr. Hyde I could be more blunt. In each situation, there were virtues and flaws. The flaws in the Mr. Hyde situation had the advantage of being obvious; the virtues were clearly uncertain. In dealing with a Mr. Hyde of finance, it is always essential to suspect his enthusiasm;

he will always tell you the best. Usually a Dr. Jekyll will be very careful not to exaggerate the possibilities of profit; if anything, one of the elements you have to be wary about is not to be misled by his cautious conservatism. Dr. Jekylls, like fine practitioners of medicine, do not want to be criticized for exaggerated enthusiasms. If a Dr. Jekyll is optimistic about his prospects and profits, they are likely to be even better than he says. It is when things begin to go a little bit wrong that you can't be so sure.

The great respectability and probity of a Dr. Jekyll type of person, whether in Wall Street or elsewhere, can, without any ill will on his part, be misleading, and under certain circumstances tragically misleading. The fact that you trust him so much means you will find it difficult to be alert to the danger signals when they appear. His success in solving business problems in the past will make him reluctant to recognize the true extent of the unexpected difficulties which confront him. While the Mr. Hyde person will deceive you consciously, the Dr. Jekyll type deceives you unconsciously and, whereas the Dr. Jekyll type does good consciously, Mr. Hyde does his good deeds unconsciously.

The history of investment would show that far more money is lost in good investments than in bad, and more is made by the public in the dubious speculative securities than official writing on investment leads one to believe.

It has to be that way. The great mass of capital is invested in good companies, good at least in the sense of respectability, of being managed by earnest-minded, competently trained officers, of owning substantial assets and performing worthwhile services. The amount of money invested in wild ventures—unproved uranium mines, small wildcatting oil companies, a new machine for making pills—is small compared to the great total mass of investment, and not all of these wild companies are run by Mr. Hydes, nor even when they are, do they always fail. Therefore, the basic danger to society from the purposefully deceptive Mr. Hydes is small; that from the self-deceiving Dr. Jekylls is great.

What creates Dr. Jekyll and Mr. Hyde situations in economics are forces of nature. The forces are inseparable just as they are in the psychological nature of individuals—an interweaving of lauded and lamented characteristics constantly exists. The dominant traits of most people are praiseworthy—the evil person is a rarity—but the nicest people do the cruelest things; the harshest mothers and most unfeeling fathers live in the nicest houses wearing the prettiest slacks and best-looking sports jackets and pay their bills promptly. The duality of life is not confined to individual life but exists in economics too. Nor can the traits ever be separated, the duality terminated, and life, economic or otherwise, be straightened out and made all good, the way people are constantly trying to do. There are certain situations which can only be coped with by Mr. Hyde and others by Dr. Jekyll, and in all managements there is some mixture.

The actual Mr. Hydes of industry must, of course, have a great deal of the Dr. Jekyll in them because they deal with a large assortment of human beings who are, quite naturally, for the most part, of the Dr. Jekyll type. And the gifted and celebrated Dr. Jekylls of industry must have sufficent of the Mr. Hyde in them to cope with the Mr. Hyde aspects of the people they must deal with.

I sat with Mr. Hyde, the steel man, and his large staff of Dr. Jekylls at lunch in the club-like quarters which he had acquired for the company so that the staff of his far-flung organization and the visiting salesmen, purchasing agents, and technicians of importance could be properly accommodated. It was an excellent meal—not lushly served but

amply done. The salad was something an epicure might notice because you seldom get good salad away from a well-run
home. And the atmosphere of the place was that of a well-
run home.

I have sat with the Dr. Jekylls of the chemical company
many times in their cafeteria. They make a policy of not having a private dining room and of eating the same food as the
workmen. It was neither bad nor good, just typical low-
priced cafeteria food. We sat at an ordinary table—very
democratic and not much fun. The policy of this chemical
company was to keep the unions out and one way to do this
is for the officers to act in a simple, unluxurious, one-of-the-
boys fashion. In general, the more of Mr. Hyde there is in a
management make-up, the better the food the officers eat.
And the more there is in them of the serious Dr. Jekyll, the
more likely are they to eat in the company cafeteria.

The staff of the steel company was, as I have said, made
up of Dr. Jekylls. There was only one Hyde and that was
their leader. This, I think, is fundamental—the staff of any
organization must be made up mostly of Dr. Jekylls. Without
the large mass of their goodness, the thing would not work.
But some situations also need a Mr. Hyde, a person who
feels, understands a situation, and who can measure and
deal with things which are not so good and which would
confuse and horrify a Dr. Jekyll.

The reason Mr. Hyde took a day off to show me around
was that I was in a position to help the market for his stock.
He had now improved the plant enough so that he had a
chance to make a respectable organization out of it. A better
market for his stock would help him do this since it meant
that he could raise new capital (by selling more stock) on
better terms. I realized, of course, that a better market would
also give him and his associates a chance to sell some of their

large holdings of stock which they had acquired for very low prices when they took over the ancient industrial wreck. You can never tell for sure about the motives of a Mr. Hyde. In fact, you can never tell about a Dr. Jekyll, since Dr. Jekylls like cash in their profits too. There was no doubt, however, that this Mr. Hyde had built up his property and that the property had the inherent possibility of being built up further. Mr. Hyde could create for himself a situation in which he could, in his old age, become Dr. Jekyll, and this seems to be an ambition which all Mr. Hydes have and which they sometimes achieve.

As an initial step, Hyde had given his new tin mill an entirely separate executive department—it had its own stairway, its own paneled rooms and pile carpeting. This meant that its customers were kept separate from other buyers of steel. The tin plate was being sold at regular scheduled prices, the same as those listed by the great steel companies. The other products of the company were being sold at various prices. For customers of the region who would promise to give the company business when the boom was off, the steel moved at regular prices, but for other customers it moved at big premiums. Through changing premium prices when the market permitted and by holding back taxes due the government on these profits, the company collected capital for improvements. Uncle Sam and Mr. Hyde had, however, finally reached an agreement about these delinquent taxes. The company would have been in a tight money squeeze as they were paid off had not the steel boom proved much greater than expected.

When Hyde was taking me around his mill, we came to a spot where a soaking pit was being cleaned. These pits are where the ingots are taken out of their molds and held at high temperatures until ready for rolling on the mill. Hyde walked across the pit on a beam, saying, "You don't mind this, do you?" I did, so he steadied me and helped me over. It was patently bad procedure to allow anyone, let alone the president of the company and his cherished visitor, to walk a beam across a deep and still rather hot pit, even though the beam we walked on was wide and not very long. Modern plant practice puts a tremendous emphasis on safety, and a path like this would not be found or chosen in a modern plant run by careful Dr. Jekylls. I wondered after we walked the beam about the number of lost-time accidents in the plant. I wasn't surprised when an hour later we had to wait at a road crossing as an ambulance turned into the plant yard. Hyde wasn't concerned to see the ambulance. Physical danger or damage apparently meant little to him. Though elderly, he was strong and active. All day we kept hopping over pieces of equipment rather than taking a longer route and finally he said, "I'll make an acrobat of you yet." I felt that there was one thing that was characteristic of the Mr. Hydes (and it had to be, otherwise they would not survive) —they had to have wittiness. They are also (and have to be) courageous. But in addition they are—and I suppose this is fundamentally their chief sin—likely to be impatient and reckless.

The Dr. Jekylls are courageous too, but it's not an unexpected quality since they represent what human beings admire, including courage. They are much more sympathetic, artful, and thorough, because they have a more careful ability to visualize how one thing relates to another. But they are likely to be less witty than the Hydes. Perhaps another way to say it is that the Dr. Jekylls are more mature—in fact, sometimes frighteningly mature. The Hydes, who expect almost anything can happen, are more like children. To them cause and effect are not so definitely related. The reason they allot themselves outrageous amounts of stock when promoting a company and give the public so little for its money is not because they want to take advantage of the public's gullibility but because, to some extent, like children, the real thing is what one imagines. They are like children playing with paper money. They play with the cunning and cruelty of children too, and they can do the damage that a big child can do.

It cannot be said that man for man the Hydes have more ability or imagination than the Jekylls or vice versa. The Jekylls have a better feeling for the real existence of material things including the real existence of investors and the feelings these investors will have if they lose their money. The Jekylls are able to visualize what can really be accomplished in the tangible world of material things while the Hydes are more convinced about the true existence of the unreal and they think (usually mistakenly) that, by sheer cleverness, it can change into the real. But the reason they continue to function from generation to generation, despite all the efforts of law agencies and the agencies of respectability such as the New York Stock Exchange, is that they are partly right. New wealth is being constantly discovered or developed in places or in uses where no one thought it existed. Most of it is discovered by the powerful sustained efforts of the more imaginative of the Dr. Jekylls, but some of it, sometimes a great deal of it, is uncovered by the witty Mr. Hydes.

One of the interesting aspects of the financial district and the economic framework is the complex intermixing of Hydes and Jekylls, not only in each individual (where psychological forces corresponding to the symbols Hyde and Jekyll are always intertwined), but in the actual fabric of the personnel of finance. When you hear the Dr. Jekylls talking about the Mr. Hydes, you would think they would have

nothing to do with each other. The Mr. Hydes sound like
the Untouchables in India. But then you go to some large
industrial cocktail party, and very often the Hydes and the
Jekylls are together. The Mr. Hydes make the Dr. Jekylls
nervous, but they have, as I have said, an economic reality
which cannot be ignored.

It often amuses me to meet some important customer of
the firm, whom I had been lead to believe, more by tone of
voice than exact words, was interested only in the most respectable of financial situations, and then to find that he has
a vivid interest in a Mr. Hyde company which my wander-
ings have led me to know about. When I have written about
some Mr. Hyde situation and been criticized by a frowning
partner, I have found that in our offices there is a customer
who is heavily loaded with the stock and delighted to find
that our research department knows something about it. In
Wall Street, of course, everyone is basically interested in
money, and Mr. Hyde's stocks often can be extremely profitable, especially for those who are lucky and witty enough
to get out first. Occasionally there is enough reality in the
economic function being performed so that it becomes a big,
sound company.

The basic economic function performed by the Mr. Hydes
is to create an economic opportunity which would not be
created by the Dr. Jekylls. The steel company had been sold
for junk by the big industrialists after the war. It is very
unlikely that anyone but a Mr. Hyde type of industrialist
would have been able to believe it could be built up again,
or would have wasted time trying. The really able Dr. Jekyll
industrialists had better things to do; the less imaginative
Dr. Jekylls would not care to take the risks which are clearly
inherent in a very dubious industrial situation. It takes a
certain combination of detachment from reality and real

constructive ability to do the jobs that the Hydes do. There can be no doubt that the steel company had a useful economic function, melting a million tons of steel a year at a time when steel was short and many businesses hampered because they couldn't get metal to work with. It was high-cost metal, but for the man who needs to build something, the cost of having steel is much less than the cost of not having it.

The facilities were old and relatively inefficient, but to duplicate them in a modern plant such as the Dr. Jekylls of finance would approve of might have cost $250,000,000. But the normal list price of steel was not high enough to pay for this sort of investment. In an economic sense, goodness was not good enough to supply the steel which Mr. Hyde, with his not entirely good intentions, was supplying. Only one completely new steel plant had been built in the United States since the war because the normal list price of steel had not been put high enough to make investment in a completely new steel plant worthwhile. Failure of the steel industry to put its prices high enough to pay for adequate new investment in plant represents an economic sin of considerable magnitude perpetrated by the great and good Dr. Jekylls of finance. This failure was translated into shortages of steel and a resultant loss of business, jobs, and take-home pay, by those who used it.

The sins and wickedness of the Mr. Hydes are obvious and relatively lacking in real economic danger; those of the Dr. Jekylls are unconscious and subtle and capable of great economic damage. One of the fixed beliefs of the Dr. Jekylls of economics is that low or at least stable prices are good prices. Whenever the price trend rises, you see the banking and governing authorities getting all a-flutter because they think a rising price trend is inflationary and therefore bad.

But rising prices can be good because they stimulate investments in new enterprise. In the case of steel, prices had been kept too low for decades because the officers and directors of the U.S. Steel Corporation, which completely dominates the policies of the industry, have a turgid fear of political criticism from Washington.

Steel is not the only product which has historically been priced too low. Nickel is another example. In order to prevent competition, the International Nickel Company held the price low. Nickel scrap has sold as high as $3.50 a pound while, at the same time, pure, new, virgin nickel has sold at 60 cents a pound. Those who were not old customers of International Nickel had a hard time getting any, and those who years ago were not important customers because they were then small had a hard time getting enough to support their developing businesses. This meant that new or growing companies had to buy high-priced scrap. If International Nickel had put the price up years ago to the real economic value of the metal, other, higher-priced mines, working with poorer but nonetheless usable ore, would have come into being. International Nickel would have made more money during good times, but there would have been more severe dips during recessions. The pricing policy of the company was probably well intentioned, at least in some respects, but analysis of its total effect shows that it hurt as much as it helped. It affected not only various companies which would have liked a more generous supply of nickel as an alloying material but the national defense effort since it made nickel a scarcer commodity than it would have been had the price been higher.

Just as the ex-bootlegger who helped finance Mr. Hyde's steel company grew rich because of the error in goodness which led millions of well-meaning Dr. Jekylls to vote for

Prohibition, just as he performed a virtuous function without perhaps having particularly virtuous intentions, so this steel company survived and grew because of the big, elemental sin of the leaders of the industry.

Throughout industry, you will find there is virtue in Mr. Hyde and sin in Dr. Jekyll, and often one exists because of the other. I know dozens of examples—a new way of making gelatin capsules for drugs, a new way of prolonging a medical dosage, a new type of fire extinguisher. I had them checked by good Dr. Jekyll technicians and concluded there wasn't enough virtue in them, but there was some merit, and they would never have had a chance if some Mr. Hyde of finance had not sold stock to the public, to give them a start. And I am not the final judge; the merit in the typical Mr. Hyde company is enough to keep it functioning for years and some finally break through to become strong. The prospecting of one of the really great uranium areas in North America was financed in its early dubious days by one of the best-known Mr. Hydes of the financial district. After years of being no good to anyone but himself, he found an economic virtue big enough to more than balance his sins, and he has now become one of the most respectable of our Dr. Jekylls.

Whereas the virtue of the Hydes is that they are not greatly impressed by what is called reality and give almost anything a chance, especially if a small part of the chance can be sold to the public at a good price, the sin of the Jekylls is to be overimpressed with reality, to feel that it is more fragile and precious than it is, and to want to establish a status quo for it. This status quo is not intended to be one of stagnation but one which makes orderly, controllable progress. It is a pretty pattern, but because of the existence of cosmic intangibilities which constantly, and not in orderly ways, change into tangibilities, it is a pattern which cannot really develop. In all things economic and otherwise, it remains a fantasy of the respectable. It can have a charm but not a reality. It is a strange thing, this respect for reality which the Jekylls have which turns reality into a fantasy which has not only a charm but a dangerous insanity about it. These sane people never recognize their insanity no matter how many generations there have been or how much they have read about their past.

Most of us are Jekylls—controllability, orderliness, and comfortable progress mean a great deal to us. But there is a sin in wanting them too much. Severe punishments have been meted out throughout history to those nations, companies, or families who have loved tangibility and wanted to control and husband it too much.

For the investor, it is not so important to realize that there is virtue in the Hydes as that there is sin in the Jekylls. Most investors will not be waylaid a great deal by a Hyde. Most of them can sense the exaggeration, the inaccuracy, and the improbability of the claims which the Hydes of finance make for their securities. The very printing which goes into the promotion of a Hyde type of stock, the paper chosen, the type face as well as the phrasing of the words shows the kind of effort. An investor who buys a stock from Mr. Hyde usually knows he is taking a gamble. The price of the stock, which is always low, and often measured in dimes or nickels, indicates that. It is true that many people who take gambles are very poor gamblers. When things go wrong they realize then that this wasn't really what they wanted to do. But their anguish at losing does not belie the fact that they knew at the start they were not dealing with a high-class situation. And some of the Hyde situations turn out to be good, which is what makes the gamble worth taking.

The total amount of money put into Hyde situations is small. In the whole steel industry, there are three Hyde type of stocks that I know of. The total market value of their shares as I write this is $80,000,000. The total market value of U.S. Steel Corporation's common stock is three billion dollars. Whether the management of U.S. Steel runs the company with real virtue or succumbs to the sins of industrial piety is much more important to the economy of the whole country and to investors than the fact that there are Hydes running the three small companies. I have before me the promotional literature of one of the Hyde companies. Knowing this company well, I can only shake my head at the way the "facts" are presented. I read these lines, printed in modest type, at the bottom of the last page:

We believe in the future of this company and maintain a trading position in this stock.
Independently thereof we may also maintain a small investment position.

This "small" investment position which they "may" maintain was undoubtedly given to them either for free or at a price much below the market as payment. Sinful, for sure, but since the company does have a thousand men working for it and is earning good money, and since its president, in this case a young man, does work and drink hard for the benefit of the company, the sin probably isn't very great. In fact, it may be no sin at all. The stock probably is worth, on sound economics, what it is selling for, and by promotion, the company probably can be built up to greater strength.

But in an annual report of U.S. Steel, which never would give any tipping service an under-the-counter deal in its stock, there is in my opinion a bigger sin. There is a discussion of economics which displays deep hostility toward the unions on the part of its management. The discussion is of dubious merit from the point of view of economic theory and the hostility displayed toward labor cannot do the corporation or the industry any good. An important investment counselor asked me what I thought of this section of the report which created quite an unpleasant stir in the industry, and I said, "It did not have in it the inherent possibility of doing the stockholders any good."

The sins of the Hydes, like all sins of a recognized criminal character, are small in scale but definite, picturesque, and easily described. The sins of the Jekylls represent much deeper weaknesses of humanity: complacency, arrogance, conceit, and a desire to rule and benefit by power of position and law rather than by power of continuing creativeness. These are common and also commonly well-veiled weaknesses of most of us. They are, as time marches on, our undoing. Perhaps the worst sin of all is to think we should not be undone. Perhaps the great virtue of the Hydes is that they are doing things for which often they should be punished and they live in the expectancy that some day they will be caught up with. The Jekylls have the illusion that they are always doing something for which they should be praised and they should never be caught.

CHAPTER FIVE

Sexual Forces in Economic Actions

There is one earth but two worlds—one, the world of men; the other, the world of women. Everyone who has grown up knows from experience that these two worlds have areas of ambition and experience in common, but also large areas of difference.

Economic actions are made up of the total of two grand forces—the male and the female. The male force, however, is much more recognized in terms of money than the female.

Men are, to a large extent, paid for what they do. If they achieve certain types of eminence they can be very highly paid. Women are, to an equally large extent, not paid for what they do. Women who are considered in their community remarkable, as women, get no extra pay for it. In fact, one reason they have such a high rating as women is that they do so much good for the community and get nothing but praise.

Women could be paid for their activities as women. If a woman cleans an office building at night she is paid. The work she does is very similar to what she does when she goes home. But for that she is unpaid. No one would argue that keeping a home livable is less important than neatening-up an office, but one is a paid activity, the other taken for granted.

There is no purely technical reason why women could not be paid for their own housework. We gave G.I. bonuses to about 15,000,000 men. This was a crude effort at mass evaluation of services for which monetary values in detail have not been established. Women could be given bonuses for being housewives. It is not likely that this will happen, though such a proposal has been made in Britain by some Scotch members of Parliament. But if it did happen, it would clarify one of the aspects of sex as it affects economics.

The unpaid economic activity of women is, however, a real economic power. The typical activities of women, which have never been and may never be paid for, produce wealth just as actual as the paid activities of men.

Because women are unpaid, the economic vigor of every country is substantially underestimated. The estimates of economic power which appear in official statistics are confined to those which are paid for and also to those which the law approves of. The dollars paid Polly Adler's call girls did not find their way into the estimates of Gross National Product of 1929; neither did the millions of dollars paid Dutch Schultz or Al Capone for bootleg liquor. However, the salaries paid cops to arrest the call girls or close an occasional speakeasy were. The economic activity of the Prohibition era was undoubtedly underestimated because of the Puritanism of our statistics. The production of steel, oil, and coal, the manufacture of automobiles, transportation by air and rail, the maintenance of buildings, provision of commercial amusements—all such activities find reflection in official national income statistics; but most of the work of women, legal or illegal, does not.

If a country produces steel or oil in small amounts, as China did until recently, the official figures give it a low national income. But it is obvious that such statistics are somewhat lacking in significance. The Korean war proved that we did not have the easy, overwhelming power that the comparative statistics indicated. There are more human beings living in China. The Chinese armies, drawing on this huge supply of young men, held us down in Korea. The production of men in China plus the production of arms in Russia made China a great military power. China was far stronger than the statistics made it appear because of the economic force of women.

The power of women to produce children is not counted (except in some countries to a minor degree) in monetary terms as among the assets of a nation, yet everyone knows that this is among the most vital of powers. And, also, the full power of a nation like China to feed its millions is not counted. Home gardens are part of the national wealth of both America and China, but in China they are relatively more important than in America. Home gardens or family-sized farms are, in considerable part, a product of women and their households. Most American agricultural production shows up in statistics—we look strong. But could we feed 600,000,000 people? Turning rice into people is just as potent an economic feat as turning corn into hogs. The "corn-hog ratio" is part of the lingo of economics. The "rice-child ratio" is something an economist can't evaluate as clearly—not as yet, anyway.

Whoever molds national policy has the problem of estimating as correctly as possible the relative strengths of different nations. The strengths of nations include social strengths, spiritual strengths, and economic powers. A contribution of an economist to national policies should be a realistic estimate of economic strengths. Because economists focus their attention on the productive powers of men—which is reasonably well established in terms of money—and ignore a large part of the productive power of women because it is not reflected in monetary terms, they have been arriving at consistently unrealistic estimates of the relative national powers.

For instance, the per capita personal income of China is estimated by United Nations' statisticians at $27 a year, that of the United States at almost $1,500 a year. An American apparently has more than 50 times the economic power at his command compared with the Chinese. But these estimates very largely reflect the work of men. Suppose we make, informally, an estimate for what the women contribute and add this to the estimated per capita income of each nation. Since women's work is more similar throughout the world than men's, an estimate of the national contributions of women should not vary so much as that of men. If housework were put on a U.S. minimum-wage basis for theoretical calculation, the per capita income in the United States might be increased about $650 a year, that of China about $500 a year. This revised Chinese per capita income of $527 would still be smaller than the American of $2,150 but the significance would have narrowed. It would make the American economy look only four times more powerful than the Chinese, which seems more reasonable.

If an attempt to pay real wages for what women do as women were to be made, the politicians and the economists would run into trouble. It is one thing to recognize that a woman cleaning her own house is doing just as valuable a job as when she cleans an office building; it is another to actually pay her for it. If the 60,000,000 housewives of the nation were to be paid $1.25 an hour for their work at home, the national house-cleaning bill would come to $75,000,000,-000 a year. And this would be pay for only 40 hours a week. Obviously, women might not feel they were being adequately paid for what they were actually doing. The rate of pay would, moreover, be at the minimum rate per hour. It would represent no recognition for unusually competent

housework or for the especially skilled elements of this occupation: cooking, treating the husband psychologically, adjusting herself to the ego demands of children of a wide
variety of ages, etc. If women's work were evaluated by
scientific time-motion studies, plus an allowance for intangibles, as man's work is, the national wage bill might become
so large that the expenses of a new global war would look
like a bargain.

But if women once realized that it was ethically and
scientifically justifiable to be given some recognition of their
labors in monetary terms, they would want it, and I imagine
that, some day, a nation will experiment with giving it to
them.

We have to remember that there was a time when most
work went unrecognized in monetary terms. For the greater
part of the world's history men have delved and women
spun. Human concepts of economic possibilities have been
very similar to animal concepts. An animal merely seeks to
live (a very worthwhile objective). And to a great extent
most people have simply worked to live. Those who lived on
a high scale did so by enslaving others. The concept that
many, and perhaps most, human beings could live on a high
scale came with the machine age. But women, until the
development of household machinery, have seldom had
slaves. A woman's mode of life is still relatively primitive.
She bears children, she nurses, she feeds, she rears, and picks
up after it all. The woman of today is much less removed
from the women of thousands of years ago than the man.

Women have been dependent on men for certain practical
things and men used to be equally dependent on women.
Children were once the only old-age insurance most men
had, and it was women who made this old-age insurance
possible. Children were also the family labor pool. But in

modern life, especially in our country, children are less important from this primitive point of view. There has been a shift of emphasis. The primitive reciprocity of men and women has been diluted by civilization. Women, for the most part, still feel in the tradition. They still feel themselves bound to men, dependent on men, as even the chattels of men. But while they feel this, they also resent it. They do not entirely like the loss of independence which comes with marriage. But they don't know what to do about it. I am not suggesting a complete cure, but it is obvious that women would take a step toward a new and more civilized reciprocal relationship if their work were evaluated in monetary terms; if, in short, they were paid at least in some measure for the functions which they now perform but are not paid for.

Such an experiment would have the practical virtue of being one way of distributing purchasing power more equitably and of stimulating consumption during one of the periodic business recessions of a free capitalistic economy. It is conceivable that a number of important social and economic problems could be alleviated by giving women some allowance for being women.

For instance, high personal income taxes are among the problems of recent years. High personal income taxes are based in part on the thought that those who are best able financially to carry the nation's financial burden should do so. It has also been believed that high income taxes are a technique for cutting down excessive private accumulations of capital and from preventing a concentration of the sources of wealth in a few hands, such as has occurred in other countries and other centuries and has injured or wrecked previous civilizations. But these graduated income taxes create new types of inequities with which we are all now somewhat familiar. Another way to accomplish at least part of the reform originally desired would be to pay women for being women. This is illustrated in the table below:

Table II.

	Rich Families' Income Before Taxes	Bright Executive Families' Income Before Taxes	Workers' Families' Income Before Taxes
Income of Man	$100,000	$25,000	$5,000
Proposed Income of Woman	2,500	2,500	2,500
Total	$102,500	$27,500	$7,500

While giving women who are married to men of different income levels equal recognition for their contribution as feminine personalities would not equalize family income, while it would leave the competitive pattern of our society in existence—it could contribute toward bringing families nearer together and placing a value on family life which is more in keeping with women's real contribution. It isn't necessary in order to maintain a free and productively competitive society to have the competition stated in terms of man's type of work only. If we are going to have a free competitive society it should be a society in which the true productive powers of different individuals are valued as accurately as possible.

At present too much recognition goes to men, and also men working in certain occupations. Our society is not as competitive as it seems. The great differences in personal incomes make it look extremely competitive, but actually a certain type of man perpetually acquires more than his share, and puts himself and his family in a non-competitive position compared to others. For instance, we give salesmanship a very high monetary value. A really good salesman can earn a huge income and give his children every advantage of health, education, travel, etc. We give teaching a very low monetary value. A really good teacher may have a hard time giving his children food, let alone a really good education and much travel. In the town in which I lived where more is paid per pupil for education than in any other town in that state, the teachers have to take jobs as garage mechanics, waiters in restaurants, postmen, etc., in order to come anywhere near giving their families the life which every American considers desirable. This just doesn't make sense. Giving women some recognition for their existence would be one technique of making better economic sense than we do.

Or let us take the case of a geologist I knew—he found one of the world's greatest deposits of iron ore: the huge trough now being exploited in Labrador. Sitting at Ruby Foo's in Montreal, I asked him what he had gotten out of it. "Just my salary," he said ruefully. Only then did this scientist realized that in choosing honor he had left millions—literally tens of millions—to the financiers and promoters who knew how to choose money. They will have honor too—watch the obituary and society columns. Their children won't have to compete economically in our society; the geologist's will.

But while monetary recognition of woman's economic force is desirable, it would be just a superficial recognition and would represent a merely superficial understanding of the sex force of the female as it affects economic action.

The great power of woman is primarily the power both of giving life and of giving pleasure to the life she gives. To an economist this creative power appears still to be merely a conventional economic factor. He does not appreciate the economic implication of its psychological dynamics. He gathers statistics on the birth rate and the rate of new family formation and figures out how many customers there will be for a chain store 15 years from now. He advises a local school board as to what they must provide for. He may then advise a building supply company as to what they can hope for in the way of a market from towns which have to build more schools.

What artists understand and what economists do not is that a woman is a composition. Both psychologically and physically, a woman is a play and conflict of forces. It is the play and conflict of forces within a woman, reflected in the contrasting forms of her body, which makes her fascinating in herself. It is this fascination with herself—not a vain fascination, but a lucid one—which contributes to her fascination for others.

A man is not fascinated with himself; he is fascinated with action, and especially with actions which are involved with the discovery of things he did not know existed. A woman's discovery is the bringing out of things which she knew existed. Neither men nor women are ever completely satisfied by their different types of discovery. A woman's dissatisfaction is somewhat like looking in an attic. She feels sure that something is there which she has not found. The acts of sex and the birth of children temporarily reassure her, but there is always something she is looking for left in the attic. A man is primarily interested in how a woman works. That is the great mystery to him. Time after time a woman will pass by, but each new woman has a good chance of twisting his head. Science and religion are largely sublimations of this unsatisfiable curiosity of men. Women do not need explanations; they are well satisfied by life, providing they can experience enough of it. Women want to live, they are satisfied by results, and men want to find out how things work.

The advance of civilization has consequently not made

woman any happier than she was, or any less happy. Navaho women, living in the ancient hogans of the Southwest, very much as their ancestors did thousands of years ago, are neither more nor less happy than the women of Park Avenue. They would undoubtedly have the bright intelligence to shift quickly to Park Avenue duplexes if their husbands found an oil well, but their emotional patterns would not change; they would carry them within themselves.

There is nothing men can do, outside of being men, to make women happier, or less happy, but women will enjoy watching them try because, whatever men do, women will enjoy watching them do it. Men's striving is one of women's delights.

Women have an intense admiration for men—an admiration based to some degree on the practical necessities of life but to a much larger degree on the psychological necessities which stem from being a female. And also there is nothing women can do to assuage the dissatisfaction of men, to make them content, as women are, with the actual living of life.

The complexity of human life arises out of the simple physiology of sex. But the physiology of sex, while simple in its obvious differences, causes complex and unending psychological reactions. The impact of early observation has been explained by Freud. Unfortunately, few people yet understand the full force of these complexes, their full necessity in creating human personalities, and their far-off ramified effects in the fields of politics, economics, etc.

The satisfactions women have with men, plus their ability to derive pleasure from the complex but if need be inexpensive experience of life, poses one difficult economic problem. Wealth cannot mean much to women except through complex psychological association. A woman can be made deliriously happy with a present of a box of hot nuts which her man, poor in money, an inefficient, irascible idiot when it comes to job holding, but nonetheless her man, brought to her. If he had more money, it would have to be a larger present, but it is the thought that counted; that old phrase can be the real truth. Women, therefore, may be inclined to put up with a bad economic system because poverty hasn't brought them personal unhappiness. They may not see that rebelling against their economic lot has a practicality which would make them any happier.

One of the great unstudied areas of human action is that of social revolution. Is it true that poverty breeds revolutions? It is generally accepted that poverty sparked the French and Russian Revolutions and also the Communist success in China. However, poverty did not breed the American Revolution nor the Cromwellian revolt in England. The leaders of both Anglo-Saxon upheavals were prosperous men. Washington and Jefferson were millionaires. As for the French Revolution, the researches of Professor J. U. Nef [1] throw grave doubts, to say the least, on the popular fable.

Nef is one of the leaders of a small group of scholars who has been actually looking at the production statistics of past centuries. The statistics of France suggest that that country was enjoying an unprecedented industrial boom when the fighting broke out. In the early part of the eighteenth century, France had been a backward country compared to England. However, in 1715 the rich coal fields along the Belgian border were discovered. French coal production increased between 600 per cent and 900 per cent by the time of the Revolution. Iron and steel production also spurted ahead, and France caught up with and was well ahead of England by the time Marie Antoinette went to the guillotine.

[1] J. U. Nef, *War and Human Progress* (Harvard University Press, 1950).

One of the curiosities of the human thought process is its tendency to ignore very simple but significant statistical indications. Napoleon himself said, "God is on the side of the heaviest artillery." Napoleon could not have had this divine power on his side unless France had had Europe's greatest industrial machine. France therefore could not have been as poverty-stricken as romantic historians led us to believe. Simple deduction from obvious facts should have led them to conclude that the Revolution was a manifestation of rising prosperity and not abject poverty.

I don't know the statistical facts of the Russia of 1916 or China of 1950, but I suspect these facts show rising industrial power in each nation. I suspect that revolutions represent a growing tide of power breaking against an old breakwater of tradition. In countries where there is no rising tide of wealth, revolutions in my opinion do not occur. The women of such countries find means of being happy and of making their families happy despite hopeless poverty. It is only when hope rises that they encourage their men to revolt. Women always have been the great strength of suppressed peoples. Where people are poor or in difficulties, women are likely to be stronger than men. Among the poorer groups in our country the women are far more alert and sophisticated than the men. The great personalities of the Negro race have a heavy percentage of women. This is because Negro men as yet have not found a route to noble opportunity in terms of our century. In our century the noble mind among men is the scientific mind. Negro men have not yet entered the front ranks of science—but they will. Negro women have long since entered the very front ranks of women. This is because the great resource of women is not part of the conventional economic resources of a nation. Women are not impoverished when a people are poor. When a nation is rich, then the men become dominant. Man's vigor is stimulated by freedom to act. The chains of poverty really do weigh on a man. If a woman is enchained, she makes a slave of her master. Women will help men bear the burden of poverty so long as there is no help for it. Centuries will pass by, the injustices of the social order will remain uncontested. It is only when women sense that there is a practical possibility of improvement that they will encourage their men to take action.

The satisfactions men have with discovery also put a limit to the value of economic achievements. His "first million" delights—but after that he must discover again. Many men are happier going back to their offices than to their vacations. Action is a man's greatest road to happiness because it is the clearest road to discovery. Why should men want to build a space ship and brave the dangers of the cosmos? They do.

There is one thing that great philosophers have never understood about women, and which I discovered coming out on a train late at night. Women will listen to any man talk. He doesn't have to be wise—he just has to be a man they like. All the great philosophers have had their women who listened to them. They thought they were listening in admiration of the wisdom of what they said. They didn't realize that women love to see other living things in the act of being happy. A woman, therefore, likes to hear a philosopher talk. But while all great talkers had their devoted women, every other man, no matter how boring his conversation, has also had his devoted woman. When he talks, she likes to listen because it also makes him happy.

Whether the woman is a whore, a housewife, or a young teenager just learning about love, she is happy if she feels she has somehow given some type of pleasure and unhappy if she has not. A prostitute is not totally satisfied by the money she gets; she wants to give pleasure also. Not to succeed in this makes the face of a prostitute fall. All women feel that they are failures if they do not create happiness. This is not simply because they are so sweet. It is because they feel they lack something. They admire man because they do not feel any essential lack in him except happiness, which they supply. They learn the power of playing on the emotions. Deliberately they will make a person feel bad—so that later, if they wish, they can make him feel good.

One of the reasons some women become prostitutes is that the pay becomes a symbol of the pleasure they can give. The analysis of the psychology of a prostitute has always been, I am sure, much too simple. There was a school of thought that prostitution developed out of economic necessity. But prostitution continues in the U.S.A. under conditions of generally high employment. So it isn't always grim necessity. Or prostitution has been traced to neurotic problems, to nymphomania.

But what is a neurotic problem? What is a nymphomaniac? A neurotic problem is not a simple thing like appendicitis. It is a result of the power of psychological forces. Nymphomania is one of a number of possible final results of the powerful early trauma experienced by all human beings and described by Freud. It is no doubt a misfortune. Prostitution is an undesirable way of life. But a prostitute can also be looked upon as a symbol of something more important than herself.

Artists have always known this. The union between prostitutes and artists and writers is a deep one. This is because prostitutes are a link between the separation of men and women. A prostitute is a woman who fully surrenders to men. What she demands of a man is not a great deal and it is well defined. Because of this clear definition she becomes less mysterious than other women. She frees men of all obligation except the simple one of paying her, and by being so simple she becomes something like a man. She is matter of fact. Of course, in becoming so simple she is robbed of some of the mystery of a woman. The relation is both less puzzling and less passionate. A prostitute is not a normal woman, and a normal woman cannot be understood fully by acquaintanceship with prostitutes. Moreover, a prostitute quickly reverts toward the status of a normal woman if a love relationship develops.

Prostitution exists in part because it is a vehicle toward understanding, but the gap remains. A prostitute is a woman who is remarkably unsure of herself, who needs the constant reassurance of men, who must constantly conquer and temporarily acquire them by pleasing them and who, like the men themselves, is never fully satisfied by the possession in sex of the other. Prostitutes and men are thus united in a common psychological search.

In every woman's psychology there is a feeling of insufficiency, that she is not as good as she ought to be, and when she is united with a man and gives him pleasure she feels, for a while, as good as she ought to be. Every relationship of a woman with a man, or a woman with any living thing, or even with inanimate things, which to some extent she makes into living things, has this element of desiring to prove to herself through giving pleasure that, despite her deficiencies, she is good.

It is this desire to give pleasure which is the reason for her great economic force, the force not stated in terms of money. She does not demand specific recognition, because that would dilute her ability to give pleasure. Her psychological position is extremely subtle because she would like some recognition but not so much that it would neutralize her generosity. And this desire to give pleasure, to appear perfect and adorable, is based on intense fear that something has been taken from her, that she is not made as perfectly as a man. Women's amazing love of clothes, her real dependence on them for reassurance, and her consequent insatiable determination to acquire them, can be understood by economists if they understand the complexes out of which woman's psychology is formed. And with clothes go all the other things—household furnishings, automobiles, travel, which in various ways become associated with her personality. Woman is a great consumer out of psychological need.

An understanding of the psychological pressures which make women great consumers can be put to practical use as I have found from personal experience. In the spring of 1949 the stock market was hovering around its postwar lows —the rate of operations of the giant steel industry had plunged from 100 per cent to under 70 per cent of capacity. All the symptoms were assembled suggesting another typical recession.

Unemployment was increasing and economists were predicting that consumers would retrench. They predicted this because they assumed that, as workers saw other workers being dismissed from their jobs, they would fear for their own jobs and cut down their own spending. However, observing my wife and talking to many men about their wives, and being instructed in Freudian theories of psychological dynamics, I reached a different conclusion. I gradually extended my commitments in the stock market, went from a credit balance to a debit, and thoroughly enjoyed the great bull market which began to develop that summer.

I concluded from what I saw that while the typical family would certainly feel the pangs of economic fear as unemployment increased, while they would try to retrench, they would not succeed. They would not for the same reasons that I was not. Under pressure from their women they would keep on spending. The chain reaction so much feared by economists would not develop. The explosive energy of economic fear would be diluted by the psychological forces making women spend.

The ability of women to stop an economic chain reaction depends on their having enough money to spend. If for some reason there is an actual, massive ending of spending power, as there was after 1929, the propensity of women to use their money cannot dilute the forces of masculine fear. The point is that they will not fear the same consequences that men fear. Their psychology is different and, wisely or otherwise, they simply will not react along masculine economic patterns. Men will stop spending because of economic forebodings; women will shiver, but they will fear the repercussions of not spending even more. If they have the money they will spend, afraid or not.

A capitalist will stop advancing funds to new enterprise not just because he is afraid but because he hopes to gain by waiting, economically hibernating like a bear—but a woman will not. While a capitalist is afraid to lose his capital, a woman is more afraid to lose her personal attraction. Both men and women are strategic spenders, but their strategies are different.

I felt in 1949 that women would go on spending whatever they had to spend, despite their fears. They would do this not because they lacked the simple wisdom to see the grimmer possibilities in the future but because their psychology did not permit retrenchment. They were in a position similar to a fisherman who is coming home with a big catch. He sees storm clouds gathering ahead of him, he is frightened, but he can't stop his motor. And neither could he have stayed on the beach that morning when the clouds were not evident. Unless the danger is clear a fisherman must fish, and unless there is a real stringency of money a woman must spend. Economists, and most men, do not understand this. They think that women are frivolous, extravagant, and just plain unexplainable when it comes to money. They are explainable enough if you understand Freud, but they can only be explained and understood in terms of their own psychological necessities, which he discovered.

Feeling that women would surely continue to spend, I then calculated what they had to spend. I examined other economic factors to see if there was any way by which, suddenly, the money available to women could be decreased on a massive scale. I concluded that there was not—the banks would not fail as they had in 1929, thus tying up the savings and resources of millions of people; credit would not be restricted further; government spending, such as it was, would continue. I believed that the spending power of women would be large enough to buy up the inventories previously built up by businessmen and that businessmen who had retrenched because of their fear of a coming depression would have to expand again. This analysis proved correct. Moreover, the government took action to loosen credit and to add to, rather than subtract from, the spending power of women. But the defeat of a business recession in 1949 was mainly traceable to the steady spending of women. They were like the English soldiers at Waterloo. They did not falter, they held their lines and kept on spending, and they had the ammunition which was needed to win.

The economic problem of 1949 was, I felt then, very much like a military problem—the men had one strategy and concept, the women another. Each was born of their different sex-psychological patterns. Some of the men even wanted a recession because they felt it would make their money more valuable, that they could buy commodities and other men's businesses and eventually become richer. None of the women felt this way because there is nothing richer for a woman than being the maximum of herself. It was a question of which army had the greater will and ammunition. Since the men, as a whole, were not opposed to prosperity on any terms, since the businessmen who retrenched in the spring in order to save their capital were glad to expand in the summer in order to have the goods to sell the women, it was a happy victory on the whole. Only those speculators who sold short and reactionary businessmen who kept hoping for a depression were hurt.

An understanding of the forces of the psychology of sex could, of course, be put to much greater use than I was able to in 1949 if leaders of economic thought understood sex from the scientific point of view. Unfortunately, the economic theories which guide the modern world were developed before modern psychology. The great classical thinkers whose ideas still influence the economic ideology of our times—Smith, Marx, etc.—lived long before Freud. It was impossible for them to deal with sex scientifically and, therefore, they ignored it. Keynes lived after Freud, but he wrote at a time when psychological problems were still regarded as highly personal and when Freud was dubiously controversial. Freud still is controversial, many readers will think I lean much too much on him, but the proof of the pudding is in the eating. To the extent that Freudian theory explains human actions which otherwise seem strange and irrational, it has to be leaned on.

If better explanations are developed we should all welcome them, but to minimize the force of sex merely because an understanding requires a reorientation of many concepts is ridiculous. We can all observe (if we want to, but which many people don't) the tremendous power of sex, not only in ourselves but throughout nature. We don't have to look on this force romantically; we can simply regard it as a great force, the way we think of electricity. On a personal basis we can welcome it or avoid it as we wish, but we should still recognize that what we love or fear is powerful.

We should recognize the obvious, that sex splits the human race into two groups, men and women, and that these have remarkably different motivations. It is foolish to lump them together for purposes of economic theory, merely because the differences are subtle and hard to describe and understand. An economist, in order to be effective, must accept this difference and credit its importance properly. Now that it is possible to approach the problem of sex with scientific rather than romantic understanding, he must try to learn about it.

And sex, of course, is not only a question of women. Woman is the more ignored of the sexes in the field of economics, but the psychology of men is not well understood either. Businessmen think they are motivated by purely rational considerations but actually they are pushed and pulled by unconscious forces which have their origin in early childhood complexes. Few if any businessmen are prepared to understand the relationship between the castration and Oedipus complexes and an overaccumulation of inventory or general overexpansion, or the reverse—the exaggerated fear of a coming depression.

The great error which stems from the failure to understand sex is the belief in the rational. All economic systems and recommendations still have in them the concept of the reasonable being. But sex, not viewed as a romantic feeling but as a great force of nature, can be a devastating challenge to reason. The basic fault of such economic concepts is the failure to define what is rational. For instance, some economists believe in what is called a "sound money" policy. They believe the dollar should not vary greatly in purchasing power from year to year and that each dollar should have a considerable worth. For some reason they always believe the dollar should be stabilized at a level when its value was relatively high, not when its value is low. Sound-money advocates never seem to realize that what is a sound level has never been established by objective debate with dispassionate exploration of alternatives in search for a scientific conclusion. It is obvious that if you have a lot of dollars, a sound-money point of view is more rational than if you are penniless. It is more rational simply because it seems sexier to a man of established means. It is a good thing for people living on pensions, interest, or dividends to be able to feel sure that their income will have a maintained purchasing power, and it is rational for them to fight for such a setup. But how about the person with little in the way of savings? Maybe less valuable dollars but more of them would be better for him. The "sound" economist then argues that it would be better for everyone in the long run. But how long is a "long run"? Few economists have, I believe, ever run in a cross-country race. Economists seem to forget that because people die, what is good for some in the long run may be absolutely useless to others.

Then there is the opposite school which believes problems can be solved by gradual, continuous inflation. I am more sympathetic with them than with the sound-money school, but here too it is forgotten that reason starts with people's pleasure. People are never irrational if you know what their real motives are, but they often appear irrational if you ex-

pect them to reason from a certain, prescribed group of
motives. The inflationist school can't keep in its head the
simple fact that certain groups are much more favored by
inflationary tendencies than others. The worker belonging to
an aggressive labor union keeps up with inflation, may even
get ahead of it. The white-collar worker falls behind. The
owner of valuable natural resources, the aggressive speculator who borrows money and buys up real assets think inflation is wonderful. The businessman who has to pay more
for his steel, copper, newsprint, etc., and who, perhaps, cannot for some reason pass these increases along, has a different
point of view. Freudian theory teaches that people are not
abstractions, that they have intense, individual desires for
pleasure, that these desires are infinitely complex and the
decisions and efforts they make to achieve some desires may
well conflict with other decisions made to achieve other desires. This desire for pleasure in all its ramifications is the
result of sex. It is foolish to think that any thought or action
occurs which does not find its ultimate source in some phase
of sex. This is because life and sex are inseparable. But sex
is not unified—in us it is split into male and female. Therefore every thought and action is in some way conditioned by
this essential cleavage. The greatest of all pleasures comes in
those occasional moments when this cleavage seems about to
end in union.

Viewed in the light of the "pleasure principle," every
human decision is rational, though many may later prove
miscalculating and unwise. Human beings do not necessarily clearly understand what their desire for pleasure really
is. Therefore they frequently do things which are not wisely
considered. But they are always trying to achieve ends which
are desirable to them. Since the effort to achieve pleasure is

rational, a decision which leads to an eventual mishap may have been wise when it was made.

If economic theories had been constructed with an understanding of sex, and with an appreciation of the power of the pleasure principle which is inherent in the force of sex, they would have fitted the actualities of human life much better. But until very recently such an understanding of sex was not possible. Therefore we have inherited a vast mass of theory which is related to human nature the same way that the astronomical theories of the Egyptians were related to the actual universe. They were good for the state of learning at the time in which they were constructed, they contained a measure of truth, but they had no chance of leading to a comprehensive understanding of reality.

The failure to include an understanding of sex is a major flaw in both the classical communist and the classical capitalist theories. Leaders of thought in both the East and West will either have to recast their ideas in line with newer understandings of human nature or rationalize the discrepancies between theory and practice as they appear. Such rationalization has been and will remain for long the popular practical procedure. It will be a long while before economists decide that the force of sex can be understood or at least adequately appreciated and incorporated in their science. Those few businessmen and economic experts and also investors who do somehow reach an understanding of this will, from time to time, have a worthwhile advantage over those who don't.

CHAPTER SIX

Women and Wall Street

As a Wall Street professional, I have found women easier to handle than men because women will depend on you, whereas men want to give you their ideas. In any advisory situation, the best results come when the professional can exercise his gifts—whatever they may be—with minimum interference. The problem of women in Wall Street is that of women in many other situations: it is a problem in picking men.

From one point of view, women should be thought of as a symbol of the general public. Like most women, many men should be guided by professionals if they are to invest successfully. All those who are not in a position to take an active role in investigating investments must take a passive role and trust to the judgment of someone else. Women, however, differ from men in that they enjoy the passive role. They seldom question what I do, ask why I bought or sold, and they are happily satisfied by results which I sometimes think are not better than fairly good. A woman is not particularly interested in comparative results; she does not wish to know whether she did better than someone else. In any situation, investment or otherwise, she wants results which are satisfying to her personally.

Men, however, even when they are forced to be in a passive role, have a certain wish to be active. A man begins to wonder whether he is doing any better with me than he would have had he simply invested in the Dow Jones Averages. Men who know anything at all about the market will wonder if their investment advisor is keeping up with the averages, and if he is keeping up, why he isn't bettering them.

Women will be delighted if the investment advisor is keeping up with the averages. They pay him to know about things which they might know themselves if they tried, but they don't want the strain which goes with trying. A woman's attitude toward her investment counselor is just like her attitude toward any man—she doesn't demand that he be a hero; she wants him to perform a certain masculine function and leave to her the maximum opportunity to be feminine. A man, however, being masculine, wants a little touch of heroism in his counselor.

One of the misunderstandings of life is that men think women want them to have special gifts. A woman selects a man to play a role in the development of her life which may or may not include a desire to have him photographed as a hero. She often passes by men of special ability to pick one of ordinary attainments because she finds he fits the role she wants. A man will find that he has special gifts for the woman who has selected him. Similarly, an investment counselor of ordinary attainments becomes one of special ability to the woman he serves.

Women's ambitions in finance as well as their growing importance as investors has unconsciously been molding new standards of conduct and new goals of achievement for corporations and for the stock market. Some companies have been women's companies for a long while. The American Telephone and Telegraph Company is perhaps the outstanding example—it has paid dividends without interruption for over 50 years, and it paid the same annual three-dollar dividend for more than a quarter of a century. It raised the dividend in 1959, thus breaking part of a long tradition, but its management hopes to keep the other part—that of never lowering a dividend rate that has once been established. If it succeeds in this objective over a long period—say the rest of this century—its stock will clearly be a remarkable investment; it will provide a sound foundation for many people's incomes and it will also provide hope of increased income. In other words, it will provide both security and hope for more than security.

The very word security has a more dynamic meaning to a woman than to a man. To the extent that Wall Street is able to answer women's wishes, it will develop patterns of prices, earnings, and dividends which are secure.

The basic reason why women have a great fondness for security is because they have such exciting inner lives that a placid exterior atmosphere is essential to their satisfactions. It is fascinating to watch the joy that women can take in leisure—having breakfast in bed, sleeping late, taking a bubble bath, or having the leisure to study something (the piano, painting, anthropology) without any driving desire to become personally renowned or even professional in accomplishment. The life of a women is one of deep though decorous excitement. If the decorousness of a woman's life is interrupted, the pleasure in her excitement may end too. It is more important to a woman to have a secure sort of exterior pattern so that her inner enterprises can go on uninterruptedly than to have a varied exterior pattern if this threatens to interrupt her main life.

Of course women will adjust themselves to undesirable variations in pattern. Also, it must be kept in mind that every man she selects and in some way possesses is incorporated into the pattern of her life. She may take pleasure in what he does because it is part of a total male character which she enjoys. In other words, the convolutions of her man form an important part of a woman's exterior life, her admiration for him and pleasure in possessing him an important part of her interior life. Even though she may wish he acted more wisely, the violence which emanates from him is not necessarily translated into terms of psychological violence to her.

Wall Street has become highly conscious of the growing importance of women as investors because a high percentage of brokerage accounts belong to women. Wall Street has long been aware that certain sorts of stocks should not be bought, at least in any great quantity, for "widows and orphans," but it probably has not thought too much about what the psychological necessities of women will mean to it and to the country over a long period of time. Wall Street had thought about women as a somewhat different type of man—something that the word itself implies. It has wondered at times whether they were going to compete with men directly for the ownership and management of financial power. Women, in my opinion, will never become important in the management of financial or industrial power. This is because management is a full-time professional job. Women by the thousands would have to give up their lives as women in order to become a direct force of importance in finance. There are exceptional women who run companies with high success—and certain industries such as cosmetics, clothing, interior decorating, and furnishings are obviously within women's natural orbit. Women have a certain admiration for those of their sex who become important in a man's world and who prove that women could, if they wanted, be as good as men. But they also suspect that the lives of women who rival men may not be as happy as those of women who accept what men have to offer.

Just as the typical feminine person exemplifies the problem in passivity of the typical stockholder, so the more aggressive woman typifies the problem of the stockholder who wants to advise management and help direct the future of the corporation. Managements make many mistakes and sometimes it's quite easy to see them. The trouble with advising management is that the mistakes rise out of the character of the individuals rather than out of lack of information. For instance, a management may make a mistake in dividend policy by being too penurious or too generous. The information on which such a decision is based is, of course, available to the company's officers and Directors. It's complex information; it takes into account recent earnings, a forecast of future earnings, the financial position of the company, and its expansion plans. Because it is complex, it isn't possible to know positively what the right dividend policy is, but, in addition to the complexity of the information, there is the psychological variety in the characters on the Board of Directors which makes the right decision even more uncertain. Some would secretly like to see the price of the stock go up; they want to increase the dividend. Others, secretly, don't want to increase dividends because of the income taxes they would have to pay. Some officers want to hang on to the money so that it can be used in the business; others believe it wise to pay it out generously so as to please the stockholders. Perhaps they feel this way not because they love the stockholders but because they want to prevent new people getting the stockholders' votes and control of the company.

It is sometimes easy for the outside stockholder to give what appears to be good advice, but this ignores the realities of the managerial situation which, in turn, is a mixture of rational and unconscious and of impersonal and personal motives. Good advice, which is also effective advice, is hard to give and generally can come only from someone who is involved in and understands the whole situation.

An individual woman may put her fortune at great risk without breaking the fundamental feminine pattern. I know a pleasant woman who made a very large fortune in the last 15 years simply because she believed in the man who was running a small company. When stock was available she bought it. When it was available the price was usually very low because the company had a hard struggle. She had no significant knowledge of the technical merits of the company nor could the man running it be said to be utterly lacking in faults. However, her faith in him was not one of shrewdly calculating risks; she put what money she had saved in the company because she had a woman's feeling about a man. Whether a woman invests in what we professionals call sound investments or in what we would class as risky speculations, she will, in most cases, invest for some sort of woman's objective. In other words, a risky investment should not be avoided by a woman if it answers some sort of woman's need. People do not necessarily invest just to make money even though this is the most clearly rational purpose. If an investment achieves some other purpose—let's say the purpose of adventure—it can be a good investment even if it doesn't make money. To be a successful investor, in other words, one must define one's objective and then achieve it.

The question is, does Wall Street understand women well enough to fully respond to their objectives? In its wild hurly-burly past, it didn't really care, but out of this past have come a substantial group of stocks which have answered the purposes of women very well. The electric utilities and the American Telephone Company are one group. There are quite a few other stocks which have answered their purposes reasonably well—for example, the chemical, the chain and variety stores, the pharmaceutical, the tobacco, and some of the food stocks. As a whole, though, I don't think that industry has thought too specifically or intricately of the nature and desires of women in forming their policies. An individual company, of course, is not always free to form its policies. What it must do is often very largely decided for it by some outside force such as a decision by the government—perhaps even, unknown to it, some secretly taken decision of some foreign government. But if we think of Wall Street not just as a symbol of a small collection of brokers but of all industry in all capitalist countries, including the interweavings of industry with government, and if we think of women as symbolizing a larger audience even than women and of their desires as meaning something more even than the desires of women, then in some way or other I think Wall Street will think more about them. For as I have said, women symbolize a passive group which an active group must take care of.

The question is why should the active take care of the passive? It is because, I think, that the active would be lonely without the passive. The satisfactions of life will, I think, have to become more personal. This is because the world has become so large that no one is remembered long or even known at all except to himself. In the small world of many years ago, the heroes stood out and were talked about for centuries. The active people then dreamed of how they would do great deeds and be remembered forever. You can see that this is the way they thought if you read the older poetry and see how the poet addresses his patron and assures him that he, the poet, would give the patron eternal life in poetry if the patron sent the poet some money. But there is no more eternal life, only the personal life remains, and this life must be the love of the passive and the active for each other. The grandiose objectives with which we are all familiar will not satisfy us. The desire of the communists to dominate the world, the desire of the anti-communists to put an end to communism, the desire of the scientists to know every single thing there is about you and put it all on tape so that a computer can think about it, the desire even to explore the universe—picturesque as it is—will, for a great variety of practical reasons, have to be modified, attenuated, or postponed. Industry will find there is a greater but charming and responsive mystery at hand. This is the mystery which women symbolize. The mystery is the whole thing—the stars are cold lights shining through it, beckoning us on, and woman is a warm thing showing it is there.

PART II

CHAPTER SEVEN

Techniques of Security Analysis

Successful analysis of investment opportunities has to vary with conditions. There is no system of security analysis which is good for all conditions. This is the reason why a knowledge of analytical theory may prove frustrating. You get the impression, when you read any book on how to operate successfully in Wall Street, that the author has found a system for success. Then you try to apply his system and it doesn't work too well. Why? Well, for one thing, the method the author had developed out of his experience may not apply well to the conditions of the market at the time you, with little experience and a textbook in your hand, enter it. Then, too, the author is an experienced operator. There are always subtleties in a practical situation which are hard to describe and the student often misses these until he has enough experience to have a better understanding of what the book said. By that time he too has become an experienced operator and not a student. This does not mean that books and courses on security analysis have no value. They have about the same value that books and lectures on how to draw or how to paint have. You have to start somewhere; if you remember that no book and no teacher can represent final wisdom, if you can take something from a book or teacher which to you represents enlightenment, then it was worthwhile. Just don't feel that you have acquired knowledge which you can screw into the market like a light bulb—what you have is a bit of understanding which may help you somewhat, sometime.

A handicap of books or courses on security analysis is that it is hard to combine them with practice. If you take a course in an art school, most of it is devoted to practice—you draw and paint. If you are trying to learn to write, then you write and the instructor guides you from what you do. It's hard to duplicate the same learning conditions in the stock market because to practice requires quite a lot of money. Yet practice in this art is essential. One of the problems is that if you start this Wall Street practice and are successful, you won't read. You're liable to become a serious student only after you have lost some money. I must admit that this is what happened to me—I felt that this was the cost of education, which it proved to be.

Some students try dry runs—they make imaginary investments and take imaginary profits and losses. That's good as far as it goes but obviously it doesn't give you a nerve test. You don't feel the same way with an imaginary loss as with a real one. With an imaginary loss or profit you make a purely intellectual decision; with a real loss you are going to be tempted to make a decision which hurts the least. And contrary to what you may have thought I might say, sometimes this will turn out to be the best decision. So the real situation is bound to be more complex and confusing than the imaginary. So one way to create a more real situation is to practice with a little money. Only don't be too successful.

The stock market is not a game, not even a very complex game the way some outsiders think: a game has rules; if you study them carefully and have a brilliant mind, you can become a brilliant player of a game, let's say chess. But the stock market is a mass of contradictions—if you approach it the way you would a game, you are going to be hurt and disappointed because what you thought were the rules, and a way which seemed to work, suddenly will not work. I once wrote in one of my Weekly Letters: "There is nothing like the ticker tape except a woman—nothing that promises hour after hour, day after day, such sudden developments, nothing that disappoints so often or occasionally fulfills with such unbelievable passionate magnificence." If you can feel about the stock market this way, you'll do well in it.

There are a number of good books to read and a number of places to take courses. The New York Institute of Finance, once connected with the New York Stock Exchange, is one of the best. While I took classes in analysis and read parts of some books, I found more of what I was after by studying accounting and statistics.

Accounting is a type of philosophy—that's what makes it so important in understanding a business and therefore in understanding a security. When you understand accounting, you realize that nothing in business is precise.

For instance, a company I know had a problem of how much profit to show for a certain year. It had gotten big enough in defense business to be subject to renegotiation by the government and it had also become big enough to want to raise money from the public to finance its expansion. It was to its advantage to show a small percentage of profit to the government, so it wouldn't be renegotiated, but it was also to its advantage to show a large percentage to the investment bankers who were thinking of doing the underwriting. The Directors debated whether to show a profit of 20 per cent, 15 per cent, or 12 per cent. If it were 12 per cent, the company would be definitely off the hook in the government's eyes but the investment bankers wouldn't give it the deal it wanted. If it were 20 per cent, the bankers would love the company but the government would be after it like the big bad wolf was after the three little pigs. You may think the Directors pretty crooked, debating how much profit they should show. If you don't understand accounting, you will think that profit and losses are definite figures the way they are in your checkbook, or ought to be, but these were all legitimate accounting choices which an eminent, nationally known firm of auditors was willing to certify. The company's ability to choose lay in the freedom it had at that moment to choose a philosophy for evaluating inventory. After it made the choice, then its moment of freedom would be over and its accountants would be forced from then on to estimate the inventory values according to the philosophy which had been chosen. It was very much like a pagan choosing a religion—if he chooses orthodox Jewish then he'll never eat bacon, if he chooses Catholic, he'll never eat meat on Fridays, until he chooses he can eat everything.

The company had worked previously on a very conservative philosophy which had led to an underevaluation of its inventory and consequently an understatement of its real profit and a saving of income taxes. This, you may say, wasn't honest either, but it's a type of dishonesty which is commonly practiced in business. Every businessman running a small, closely held company, and many running large companies, charges off everything "but the kitchen sink" in order to hold down profits and save taxes. Sometimes this is used as an excuse for unsatisfactory results. The stockholder says, "It was something surprising to see your sales go up but your profits stay still," and the officer he is talking to says, "We charged off everything but the kitchen sink." This can mean they had too much equipment in the kitchen. But it may mean that the company was engaged in some type of build-up—maybe research, maybe advertising—which will produce better profits in the future. Many years ago when income taxes were low, these expenses might have been capitalized and written off gradually as the sales developed. Today because of high taxes, sensible managements try to charge as much as they can to operating expenses.

Both types of accounting have some inherent deception in them. The old type of accounting enabled managements to overstate their earnings, make their operations look more profitable than they really were; the new type makes them look less profitable. The type of deception practiced in the old days, whether it was relatively innocent or purposeful, was inherently more obvious—anyone looking into the situation carefully probably could catch it. The new type is more subtle. Many well-meaning managements are probably led injudiciously into increasing the costs of their operations because so much of the expense is borne by the government. If they are shrewd and thrifty, then the government takes half their profits. If they're not so thrifty, then the government tax bureaus share this lack of thrift. It's much harder for the investigator to make up his mind as to what the real situation is when a company follows an accounting policy which on its surface seems so conservative.

Also, there is no way of knowing what the real value of the assets of a business, other than its cash, are until the assets are sold. They may be worth much more or much less than you can estimate, and in practical life certain assets— such as stores and equipment—are seldom sold; they are used up or become obsolete. Therefore in preparing a statement of profit or loss at the end of an accounting period— such as the end of a year—there is always a real question as to what the results really were, and even when the management of the company is extremely ethical, there is always a considerable flexibility of choice. When a management is less ethical, the flexibility is immense.

All people who are deeply involved with securities have an understanding of accounting which they either get through formal study or by picking it up over the years. My experience with observing who makes money and who doesn't indicates that you don't have to have a deep knowledge of accounting to be successful in Wall Street. But to get a good understanding of Wall Street, you do. As I have tried to say in various ways throughout the book, if money is what you are after, you can get it by being lucky. Many people throw away their luck—they are ashamed of it, feel it's unnatural and undeserved. Maybe it's undeserved but it's not unnatural—quite the contrary, it's part of nature. If you get it, in any walk of life that you're in, don't throw it away. But also remember that it really was luck; you weren't the horse that was running—you had a winning ticket.

Statistics is the other big thing to understand. Again it is big because it is philosophical. One reason that statistics are important is because the financial statements of a company as they are made over a period of years become a time series. By time series I mean that the profits, the inventories, the plants have an importance not just as a statement for one year but as something that changes—grows or declines over the years. When you study the annual statements of a company as they develop over a period of years, you begin to understand the company the way you understand something of a person whom you have known for a long while.

But statistics also relate to the whole country and to the whole world. In fact, they are more and more related to the universe. We don't know yet how the statistics we are getting from outer space will translate into ordinary values of everyday economic life.

Statistics are really the heart of our understanding of problems and situations which are far too big to be personalized. Birth statistics, for instance—we are never going to meet more than a very few of the billions of people there are in the world or to see many of the 30,000,000 new children coming into the world every year. If we just thought of them as lots of people, their existence still would be vague. But if we can think about them statistically, then they begin to take shape. As they take shape we get a feeling of what this growth of population means, of what might be done about it, which we wouldn't have if we just noticed how crowded the world was getting. Of course, experts don't agree what should be done, but the definition given by statistics enables them to visualize the problem more sensitively.

Most people think that an understanding of what statistics mean requires a very high degree of technical knowledge. What it requires is a moderate degree of technique and some very good teachers such as I was lucky enough to have. With a dry teacher statistics certainly can be dry, but with philosophic, inquiring guidance they can open up a lot of life to you—and if you are a businessman, they can give you rapidly and simply a clarity of understanding of some aspects of the future which may prove extremely profitable.

For instance, after World War II a brilliant government statistician told the steel industry that it would have to expand far beyond any capacity its leaders had ever dreamed of. The big executives of the steel industry laughed at him. I heard Dr. Bean lecture to the New York Society of Security Analysts. He said, "I don't know a thing about the steel industry but I do know statistics"—he drew a line showing us the relationship between steel capacity and the Federal Reserve Board Index of Physical Production. Then he said the steel industry would have to increase its capacity to over 100,000,000 tons. He didn't know about steel and so the steel executives didn't take him seriously—but they didn't understand statistics. He was right and they were wrong. Steel capacity is now more than 150,000,000 tons.

Accounting and statistics are obviously related, but they are also related in a less obvious way, and in either case what you really want are not precise numbers but significant numbers. Thus in the case of population statistics, it's not important to know precisely how many people there are—it is important to know whether there are more or less. The accuracy must be in terms of the significant number which shows if populations are changing and reflects, therefore, some force causing this change or lack of change. As I said before, the statistics of a company shown in its annual reports become more significant as the company's history stretches out. When you are analyzing a very large and old company like American Telephone, Du Pont, or U.S. Steel, you can learn a great deal just from the arithmetic of the annual reports. When you are analyzing a newer and smaller company, the annual reports don't mean nearly so much; in such cases it is much more important to develop personal contact with the management—see its plants and also its products if you aren't acquainted with them in the natural process of daily life. For a major professional investor it is usually thought important to combine to some degree a statistical route to understanding and a personal visit route. To the extent that you are not going to have the time to be a relatively professional investor, your best route to understanding is through the company's annual report and through various trade publications—in general, through some sort of printed communication. Therefore an understanding of statistics and accounting would be useful to you, though if you are going to be, as most people are, fully occupied by things other than the stock market, this advice wouldn't be too practical. Still, it may give you some idea of what there is to know and to think about in this respect.

One of the mistakes people make about statistics is to think that the underlying facts they represent are as definite as arithmetic. You may see a report like this—"Employment increased last month to a new record with 67,385,000 employed—unemployment also increased, because of seasonal factors and the rise of population, to 3,826,000."

This may give the impression that everyone was counted, but it isn't so at all. The government takes monthly samplings and runs them through its formula. These samplings are carefully made but they represent only a small fraction of those actually working or looking for work. Moreover, they represent an arbitrary concept of those who want to work. If a factory is on strike, the workers are not working but they are not considered unemployed by the government. The theory is that if a person isn't looking for work he cannot be considered unemployed even if he isn't working. Also, statistics are bound to contain a sampling error—the real situation must be somewhat different than the estimated situation. The government's statisticians are aware of this and they have an estimate of the error—which, of course, is itself only an estimate. The error may be plus or minus. Thus the real employment that month may have been 69,000,000 people or 65,000,000, and the real unemployment may have been 3,750,000 people who were seeking work but unable to find it or 3,900,000. Since the average worker earns about $4,700 a year, the income available to workers that month might have been something like $1,700,000,000 or $1,600,-000,000. That $100,000,000 difference could mean quite a lot to storekeepers and tax collectors.

The uncertainty as to just how many people are working and just how much they are paid is one of the reasons why business turns out to be noticeably better or worse than the annual forecasts. There are a great many holes in our national statistics and still more in the international. For instance, the United States government does not make any estimate of the economic stature of illegal activities. Hollywood makes gangster films, but the Departments of Labor and Commerce do not make any estimates of what gangsters earn. The Monthly Survey of the Department of Commerce never says: "Income of criminals is estimated at $1,100,000,-000 last month, a rise of $100,000,000 or 10 per cent from the previous month." Yet changes in the volume of illegal activity, some phases of which are said to be very large, has an effect on our total economy similar to changes in legal activity. If gross national illegal product had a value equal to only 3 per cent of legal accounted Gross National Product, it would represent a $15,000,000,000 business—about as large as the steel business is in a good year.

Nor do we have any statistical estimate of the theoretical value of do-it-yourself activities. If you build a house with the help of your wife, the cost in money will be relatively small, but the finished house will have a normal house value if you sell it. Thus the labor which you charged up to fun can have a real commercial value. Dr. Julius Hirsch of the New School of Social Research, one of the world's most experienced economists, once estimated that the real value of goods and services created by people working on their own time and for their own use might have a value equal to 10 per cent of official Gross National Product. This would be about $50,000,000,000. The official figures probably greatly underestimate the real productive power of our nation and other nations—especially those in the Free World. It may be important to think of this because the official figures show that we are losing ground to Russia, but since the official hours that Americans work have grown shorter, we may be being seriously misled because Americans are working a great many unofficial hours doing many useful things which also are a real part of our industrial strength.

To understand our world you must remember that even when it is translated into statistics it still remains mysterious and uncertain. However, it has more of the mystery of the day and less of the night. People think that the night is more mysterious than the day—it is more fearsome, perhaps, but it is less mysterious because the blackness of night hides. The mystery of the day is greater because you can see, and each thing you see has something in it that, even though you see it, is still incomprehensible. Thus the modern world with all its education and science is more mysterious than the old world.

In general, there are three basic approaches to security analysis itself:

1. The value approach, whose high priest is Benjamin Graham and whose books on security analysis are probably the most scholarly available.

In the value approach you study all tangible factors related to a company: its balance sheets over a period of years; its reports of annual earnings sometimes called operating statements. You pay a great deal of attention to the gross value of the plant account and the annual rate of depreciation, or if you intend to be a major investor, you visit the plant, inspect it, and also to some extent inspect the inventory. You, of course, get to know the products too, and in certain cases you pay a great deal of attention to the legal position of the company—how it is regulated as to prices or profits. You do not ignore the intangibles such as what future developments may be like, but you concentrate on the tangibles in the hope that for some reason you can make your investment at what you believe is well below its true value. What you hope happens later, and this is clear and evident appearance of the true value on the market so that you can make a profit by selling to someone who for some reason hasn't had as good an eye for values as you. The value approach, in other words, emphasizes the orderly, informed analysis and interpretation of tangible assets. It tends to ignore growth as a major factor in making investment decisions. It acknowledges that growth is a true force in business but it does not make an effort to value it because it doubts that this can be done with any scientific accuracy. Basically the followers of value analysis regard the predictions of those who attempt to make an analysis of the value of growth as just another form of promotion.

You should read Graham's books in order to see what scholarship is possible on this subject. Even if you are not a scholar, you gain a sort of respect for the subject which is valuable.

2. The growth-trend approach of security valuation, which is popular and effective in the optimistic atmosphere of a long-term industrial stock market boom.

Attempts at a scholarly justification of this type of approach have been made, but it seems to me that scholarship is not the essence of this problem and the effort to make a system out of growth-trend analysis can be even more misleading than that of making a system out of value analysis.

3. Finally, there is the "be brilliant" approach which is outstandingly exemplified by Gerald Loeb in his book, *The Battle for Investment Survival*.

I have known Jerry over a period of 20 years and have seen him operate. While he has made some mistakes, he is basically very brilliant. He's a lucid, pungent writer, and his book is worth reading. Jerry has been a top broker for many years—he was one of the senior partners of E. F. Hutton and

Company before World War II and, in fact, I was a customer of his—and he is really good. The only thing is that you have to be naturally as decisive, as thorough in your own investigations, as thoughtful and as willing to change your mind rapidly as he is in order to benefit from his advice. For instance, I agree with Jerry that the way to make money is to take a decisive position, but you can also lose money by being decisive.

A few years ago he and I looked into a small research company. The market was in a bear mood and Jerry was shaking his head. He had taken a big position in New York Central, following the lead of his friend Robert Young who had committed suicide that week. Jerry said that no matter how much you know, something else sometimes happens that you don't expect and things don't work out. This was an unusual experience for him; for the most part his decisions do work out, at least so far as I can observe they do—and this is true of any successful professional. But Robert Young committed suicide. He wasn't financially broke, he was brokenhearted— perhaps because of New York Central, perhaps for other reasons. I never knew him, but Young was as ardent a student of securities as you can get. However, no matter how bright or experienced you are, how hard you investigate, how decisively you act, you are never going to be completely exempt from hazard, and if you take a decisive-enough position, the final victory may not be for you. I think that books which tell you how a brilliant person practices an art have a certain danger as well as a very real value. The danger is that you may not be that brilliant or have the same real objective. Still, the way to learn about any art, outside of practicing it yourself and learning from your own mistakes, is to be aware of what brilliant artists do.

Another thing which I do not think is emphasized by anyone writing a "how to" book on Wall Street is that a very high percentage of the fortunes made on Wall Street are made in ways which are seldom available to the average investor. For instance (as I have described earlier), my largest percentage capital gain and one of my largest absolute capital gains was made by naïvely investing $500 in a new company starting up in a friend's garage. This is not an "inside deal" of an insidious sort—you may have a similar stroke of luck—but it's not the sort of opportunity generally available. There is no sense in telling you how to do it.

If you are a Wall Street professional, there are a great many investment opportunities which come to you which are not available to the public. There is nothing insidious about these either, but they are inside deals which you can't get on the outside. For instance, I had a chance to put $5,000 in one of the first companies to make teaching machines. I had this chance because a friend of mine who was raising money for the company said, "Do you want to?" I knew nothing about teaching machines. When I saw the flimsy article they proposed to sell I would have fainted were I the faintable type. However, there was more to it than that. The educational programs developed by the heads of the new company were good. My friend and his associates guided the company most astutely and as I write this it looks as if it will be very successful, and if I estimated that my $5,000 might be worth $250,000 two years from now I would not be dreaming wildly. I got this opportunity because I am part of the professional group. I give as well as receive, and this pattern is, of course, typical of any business. The insider can do certain things the outsider can't do.

Because the United States Securities and Exchange Commission (S.E.C.) is primarily interested in the welfare of the public investor, it tries to even up the opportunities of the insider and outsider. As public ownership of securities has widened, the officials of various stock exchanges have also moved in this direction. Numerous regulations prevent us from grabbing the cream as cruelly and frequently as we used to. But even without these regulations there always have been brokers who felt it sound business to give their customers every break they could. A broker has a choice of playing a very personal game and trying to make money directly for himself, or of building a business based on doing a good job for a wide clientele. For those houses which do a big business with the public it is, therefore, good business not to be too self-centered about profits. But even so it is impossible for an outsider to be an insider. For one thing, it is the insider who usually provides the early capital for a new enterprise and the outsider is let in after the new enterprise has had a successful start and needs new capital. It is this initial growth which gives the insider the very large profits on his initial investment. But sometimes a company doesn't grow. As I write this I know of a company which is being sold for its junk value. It had the very finest sort of inside backing both technically and financially but it failed. You would have thought success was absolutely sure and you would have envied the opportunities of the insiders. The industry this company was in has grown with fabulous speed and has made fortunes for others—why did this one fail? You'll find that in Wall Street as well as elsewhere, despite the immensely acute and generally cryogenic brains which are assembled there, the mystery of life prevails. For insiders, as well as outsiders, there is unexplainable bad luck as well as good.

There is one other aspect which the books don't dwell on and that is promotion. In the old days before the S.E.C. the pithy professionals said: "Stocks don't go up, they are put up." In those days pool operations were legal and accepted by the best people as within the mores of Wall Street. It was the buying of the pools which put stocks so high in 1929 and made the crash so spectacular. Pools are illegal now and also are regarded as immoral. However, to understand Wall Street you should realize that there was an original sound and moral reason for the pools and there is an original sound and moral reason for promotion. The pools were a technique for promotion which is no longer used, but promotion goes on. It must, because it is essential for our system of enterprise. Why is this?

The average person believes that the main reason for the existence of securities is so that he can invest his savings in the industry of the country for his own benefit. He has been encouraged in this belief by the public relations departments of the stock exchanges and by the efforts of the S.E.C. and various state regulatory authorities. By now, all those people no doubt sincerely believe that the essential purpose of Wall Street is to help the public preserve and increase its fortunes. But this isn't so. The main purpose of Wall Street remains the same as its original purpose which was to raise capital for business. If businesses didn't need the savings of the public they would never sell securities to the public. There would, therefore, be no Wall Street. In a communist country there are, of course, no stock markets. Industry gets its capital from the government. In our country a tremendous amount of business is carried on by partnerships. Sometimes these become very large; sometimes they change into closely held private corporations. But in any case the public is not needed and, therefore, no stock is sold to ordinary investors.

As a whole the public plays an essential role in modern industry but it is necessary to keep in mind that the primary reason for the stock markets is to benefit industry. Originally the masters of industry had a frankly contemptuous feeling toward the public, but gradually bitter experience has taught them to be sophisticated and treat the public with a considerable degree of responsibility. Yet the old primary urge is still there. This urge is to sell securities to the public at a high price so as to raise capital advantageously. In order to do this various arts of promotion are used. Companies hire public relations experts to get their story across to as many investors as possible. They will make special efforts to interest security analysts like myself who communicate directly with investors. Luncheons may be sponsored at which company officers talk, trips to the plants may be arranged. Among the best forums from which company officers can promote their company are those of the various societies of security analysts of which the New York Society of Security Analysts is much the largest. In its early history the N.Y.S.S.A. was a highly analytical group—company officers were closely quizzed by a skeptical audience—but that was during the years when the sadness of the depression was on everyone's mind. For many years now there hasn't been too much to be skeptical about and the forums of these societies are really platforms from which a company story can be told with as much untarnished glory as a company officer wants to tell it.

Security analysts like myself, brokers, etc., have various motives for serving as part of the promotional mechanism. One is simply to do a commission business—we have to have new ideas to keep our customers. The public demands action—it wants profits. So long as the promotion is successful the public doesn't care how sound it is. Then if we help a company's stock go up, it is possible that the company will use us to do the underwriting when it sells additional stock. These underwritings can be profitable on a plain commission basis, but if the underwriter can get some options on the stock or if the company will let him bring it out at a bargain price so that he can lightheartedly keep some of it for a capital gain, it can be fabulously profitable. (I might say here that it may seem contradictory to let an underwriter bring out a new issue at a price which is sure to prove a bargain when the central motive of business is to always get the highest price that it can—but while this is a contradiction in theory it really is not in fact because in some way those managements who do a favor for the underwriter hope to benefit from the public.)

When market conditions have been good for a long while and the public feels no pain, there grows up a feeling of no regrets among many of the professionals for whatever projection of earnings or future prices they care to make. I owned a stock of a new company once which had very small sales and was losing money but which had very high hopes. I'd heard stories like this: "Flip Pills will earn five dollars a share in 1960—it's going to 100." In order to earn five dollars a share Flip Pills would have to become one of the largest drug companies in the country—a difficult but not utterly impossible task. Its management actually hoped to do this and maybe it will—but the stock went up two years before its profits. The essence of promotion isn't that what the promoters say is going to happen cannot possibly happen; the essence is that there is such a possibility but is it a probability? Promotion is the act of turning possibilities into probabilities. The promoter exudes such a feeling of confidence, his estimates of the future are not only optimistic they are so resonantly definite that all doubts in the investor's mind evaporate as a light mist dissolved by the sun thus making the beautiful landscape of the future clearly visible to the entranced eye. And the joker is that sometimes when the trance is over, the landscape really is there. If a certain number of beautiful dreams didn't turn into beautiful realities, promotion would be impossible. I have seen it happen, I have benefited from this unexpected occurrence, and I also have even seen myself lose very large profits because I thought something wouldn't happen which did.

It is because a strange magic element does exist in the development of companies, and because the public has had some experience—vicarious or direct—with dreams coming true, that promotions succeed. The essence of the whole thing is that we all can be reached by promotion—the public often in an extremely naïve way (it makes you shudder sometimes when you listen to what an average investor will believe) but the sophisticate also in a sophisticated way. Promotions affect managers of investment trusts, pension funds, trust departments. There is the example, mentioned earlier, of International Business Machines, a favorite pension-fund stock which sold for well over 600 a share in early 1961. At this price the outstanding common shares of this company were worth over $11,000,000,000, more than twice as much as all the 20 railroad stocks sell for which are used in the Dow Jones Railroad Average. These stocks included those of the Union Pacific, Southern Pacific, Atchison, Topeka and Santa Fe, and Chesapeake and Ohio railroads—all vital organizations, making money. Moreover some of the railroads own enormous assets in timber, oil, petroleum, and city real estate in addition to their rail properties. A price which values the company at twice that of these 20 railroads makes you pause. The sophisticated people I mentioned know all this—it is very easy to find out. But their sophistication does them no good. Pause to consider: "Where

ignorance is bliss 'twere folly to be wise." Many of the sophisticates follow the ignorant, but they find reasons for
what they do—elaborate, complicated reasons which if you
analyze them simply mean it has been more profitable to
invest in I.B.M. or some similar stock without any precise
justification for doing so than to buy railroads which might
easily have been justified very precisely. Their rationalization of this simple conclusion forms a sort of self-promotion
and this self-promotion, because they have enormous buying
power, naturally helps put the price up and so they find their
reasoning justified.

Most people assume that it cannot be folly to be wise—it
must turn out that ignorance is not really bliss, that the ignorant dreamer eventually wakes up and is miserable while the
wise man is blissful. This happens sometimes but many
stocks stay unreasonably high and others unreasonably low
for years on end. You may not live long enough to see either
folly, or wisdom, recognized.

Not that I.B.M. is not a great company—it is a great company; no one will deny that. The wise man tries to measure
greatness—a frequently foolish thing to do. The foolish man
may have a feeling for greatness and this feeling is frequently a wise thing to have.

There is what Freud called an "overestimation of the loved
object" in the case of stocks as well as in the case of men and
women. What you cannot love in real life, and what your
preceptors tell you you should not love in the form of fantasies having to do with beautiful ghosts of the flesh, you are
free to love in fantasies of stocks—in unmeasured dreams of
what the future may be. This dreaming comes easiest in the
case of some sort of new development. Since computers and
data processing in general were still new and mysterious to

most investors in 1961, they were free to dream of the immeasurably great things the future might bring to I.B.M. Some day, of course, this dreaming will come to an end, at least in its most lurid form; I.B.M. will join such great companies as American Telephone or General Motors or Du Pont, performing some familiar function and selling at some fairly reasonable relationship to its tangible assets and historic record.

Let's analyze this. Early in 1961 I.B.M. was selling at 67 times 1960 earnings. American Telephone was selling at 20 times its 1960 earnings, an obviously much more reasonable relationship. Each company scored new records in gross revenues and net earnings in 1960. Each is a great scientific company. Net for I.B.M. went ahead over 15 per cent in 1960 compared with 1959. That of Telephone went ahead 9 per cent. In the fourth quarter, however, I.B.M.'s net went ahead less than 12 per cent while its gross revenues (sales) rose only 7.2 per cent. Telephone's gain in gross in this quarter was therefore about the same as that of I.B.M. Its net, however, increased only about half as fast. Out of this small welter of uncertain statistics, what are we to conclude—that Telephone is cheaper than I.B.M.? That's too definite. A 15-per-cent annual increase, if it is compounded steadily, means a quadrupling in ten years—a 7.3-per-cent increase means a doubling in ten years. If I.B.M. earnings should plot out a curve of 15-per-cent compound growth in net for ten years and if investors continue to love it as they now do, then its stock will be valued at $44,000,000,000 early in 1971. It seems a little steep to me—but then the price of I.B.M. has seemed a little steep for a long while. If Telephone's net should double in ten years and the value of its stock also double, this would represent quite a bit of money too. Of course, the value of all stocks listed on the N.Y.S.E. may double or quadruple in ten years. The value of the dollar itself may go up or down—no one knows what is going to happen by 1971—and in the case of Telephone its gross revenues may quadruple by 1971 and maybe investors will fall in love with it too. The reason why Telephone's revenue might quadruple is that when computers are hitched together so that they can communicate with each other in a vast information system network, the total volume of data communication may equal the total volume of voice communication over the telephone systems. If this happens by 1971 and if voice communication over the network continues to expand at its present pace, the gross revenues of the familiar Telephone company could grow as rapidly as the gross revenues of the more mysterious I.B.M. But investors aren't thinking about this right now—they love I.B.M. It's just the way collectors love artists. Who knows what a painting is worth? You can argue about it, but can you change anyone's mind? A collector bought a painting of mine for $35 in 1960. My painting stood up in a large group show—artists I know felt I wasn't just a rich ham after all—but my paintings are not great masterpieces; they have fidelity to my personal vision but it's not a really great vision. A de Kooning of the same size would probably sell for about $10,000—de Kooning is a truly great painter—but will his painting give 300 times the pleasure, does it have 300 times the message, is it 300 times as great an artistic expression? If you are any good at all in anything, it's very hard for someone else to really be 300 times as good. But collectors think he is much, much better—and they are right up to a certain point. Beyond that it's just the happy overestimation of love. So long as the love lasts, the price stays up.

Many of those who are fortunate enough to own I.B.M.

wouldn't buy it at this price but they also wouldn't sell it because in that case they have a tax problem—taxes would eat up 26 per cent of their enormous paper profits, and this would spoil part of their illusion of wealth. The fact that investors don't sell creates a scarcity of stock which helps put the stock up to levels which are very hard to justify analytically.

In other words, once a stock goes up it tends to stay up because people do not want to sell. Even before the days of high income taxes—back when the pools were operating—a stock would tend to stay up once it was put up. This practical fact was why pools could operate. The objective of the pool members was to put up a stock and then get out. They couldn't hope to do this if there were not a natural tendency for stocks to stay up once they are marked up. People don't like to sell anything—you always find attics full of articles which have been of no use for years, and in safe-deposit boxes you find securities which have become worthless or of much less value than they once had. Their owners might have sold at one time, but for various reasons they didn't— often there was no really good reason; they just yielded to that human love of acquisition, that human reluctance to have something leave you. Old Uncle Sigmund Freud could easily tag this as the suppressed remainder of a baby-time fear—take away anything from a baby and listen to him cry— and it is the elemental human aspect of the situation which makes everyone to some degree subject to promotions. And it is the force of promotion—not statistics, economics, or any simply rational thing—that very often makes the price of a stock go up. This is something that is very hard for the public to understand. The average person couldn't understand it— otherwise promotion might cease. But even then it probably wouldn't—as I have said, we professionals not only promote, we are promoted to too. Just remember when you take a course in security analysis—if the professor doesn't tell you something about promotion, he's not telling you everything there is to tell.

CHAPTER EIGHT

Techniques of Security Analysis—Book Value

To show you by example, rather than by precept, how security analysis works, let me discuss the problem of Sharon Steel. I happen to know the Sharon Steel Corporation well, both as a physical facility and as an expression of management efforts, failures and successes, and it is this somewhat accidentally intimate knowledge which leads me to choose it.

From the point of view of "value analysis," Sharon has an obvious attractiveness. The book value of the stock at the end of 1959 was about 72, whereas the market value of the stock in the summer of 1960 was only 40. Apparently the investor had a chance to buy this stock for far less than its books say it is worth. Let us pause here and ask ourselves, what is book value?

Book value, like many other phrases of the trade, is expressive in a simple way. Every company has a set of books, and the book value is the value assigned to the assets of the company after all its debts and other liabilities have been deducted. The book value of the common stock is this value after the value of the preferred stock (if there is a preferred stock outstanding) has been deducted. There is usually the par value of the preferred, but it may be called something else. Since Sharon has no preferred stock authorized or outstanding, let's pause another moment to examine this problem and come back to Sharon later.

Suppose a company has sold 100,000 shares of preferred

stock at $100 a share, the total cost would be $10,000,000. The owners of this preferred stock would be entitled to their money back before the owners of the common got anything.

Let's suppose that this company had 1,000,000 shares of common outsanding and that its total assets, including the money raised from the sale of the preferred stock, had a book value of $40,000,000. The common would then have a book value of $30,000,000 or $30 a share. In other words, the common shareholders have a claim to all that is left after the various creditors and the owners of the preferred stocks have been satisfied.

In practical life, companies of importance are seldom liquidated. If a company goes downhill, it is usually reorganized or it is merged with a more prosperous company. In the case of either a reorganization or a merger, the claims of the debtors, the preferred shareholders (if there are any), and the common shareholders are not necessarily satisfied in the rigid order of precedence which you might think would rule from looking at the balance sheet.

Many practical considerations enter into a final reorganization or merger, which are not apparent on the balance sheet. If the common shareholders retain control of the votes, it may be necessary for the owners of senior obligations (that is the bonds and preferred) to take considerably less than they are entitled to in order to get the common shareholders to vote favorably on the plan.

My experience is that, when a company is in difficulty and when all its securities are selling low, you are better off buying the common shares at a very low, therefore highly speculative, price than investing in the senior securities at higher and apparently less speculative prices. If the senior securities are cheap, you will probably find the common stock to be even cheaper, even though it may appear worthless from a balance sheet point of view. Some good fairy always seems to rescue the common shareholders from the final bite of the hard teeth of their creditors.

Of course, this is not an inevitable rule. To make a good estimate of what sort of sick securities to buy when you are trying to make money by investing in a sick situation, you have to make a careful study of the patient company.

During the 1930–50 decades, there were scores of sick companies from which fortunes were made by various good students of financial illnesses. The leading specialist of this time as I have said was Dr. Benjamin Graham. The value-analysis technique is the way you study a sick situation and decide whether it can and how it will get well. The main reason why so much money was made by Graham and followers of his technique was that the sickness which laid so many companies low after 1930 was not that of bad management, poor products, obsolete equipment, etc., but the general sickness of the American economic system.

It was a real sickness and required real doctoring to get over, but it was the sort of sickness almost any basically vigorous company was bound to recover from sometime. A period during which there is world-wide prosperity and most companies are working and playing vigorously is not a good one for value analysis because the companies which are sick in a time like this are likely to be seriously sick.

The recession which developed during 1960–61 became quite severe for some industries. The steel industry operated at a lower percentage of its capacity during the last week of 1960 than it had in 22 years. While very few stocks sank to such low levels that they became true "value situations," many good stocks in the copper, steel, rubber, machine-tool, aluminum, and other industries got low enough so that the principles of value analysis had some use. Sharon Steel, for example, sank under 20. In general, value analysis is only applicable and therefore useful to the average investor when there has been some important type of national malfunctioning. As you can see by the example of Sharon Steel, it would have been very unwise to sink your teeth into Sharon when it was 40 in the summer of 1960, even though by value analysis it looked quite cheap. The inexperienced investor who thinks a stock is cheap when it looks cheap is almost certain to learn that it can get a lot cheaper, even if in the end it proves to be cheap when he bought it. If he borrows money to buy, he can go broke before the turn comes. On the other hand, an experienced investor often does make effective use of the principles of value analysis because he is aware of the other questions which must be considered.

Another use for value analysis is that if you are thinking of putting money in stocks and if you are worried about the boom (that is, if you think a crash or depression is coming), you may, by using value analysis, get a more vivid and specific idea of how much too high you think stocks are. If you are right in your basic premise, that a crash is coming, this extra vividness of concept will pay off handsomely. But you must remember that just because a stock sells far higher than its book value is not a reason for thinking it is too high. Book values cannot measure intangible factors, especially the immensely important factor of management. It is also not a good measure of patents which may be put into the balance sheet at cost or may have been written off entirely.

Book value is just a landmark showing you, as a landmark does from the sea, that something is there. It can be a very important landmark or it can be quite insignificant. However, discipline in the value-analysis point of view will make you question things more closely. There are lots of worthless landmarks along the borders of the seas.

The problem of what is book value and how accurately does this reflect real values has been complicated by the peculiarities of the tax laws. For instance, a company which loses a lot of money and requires a large tax-loss-carry-forward acquires, through its losses, quite a substantial asset. This is because a prosperous company may be able to merge with the failing company and use the tax-loss-carry-forward to save taxes on its profits.

A tax-loss-carry-forward works this way: Company A has lost quite a lot of money in recent years and has a tax-loss-carry-forward of $10,000,000. The managers of Company B learn of this. They are making $5,000,000 a year before taxes, but taxes, unfortunately, take half of everything they make. So they think: "If we merge with Company A, we can save $2,500,000 a year for four years because Company A has a tax-loss-carry-forward which is good for the next four years and, under the law, if we merge, this tax loss becomes ours and we won't have to pay any taxes until this carry-forward of past losses is made up."

Just what the tax loss is worth is a matter of negotiation, but it is possible that eventually the stockholders of Company A may recoup all their losses. Suppose, for instance, Company B is a brilliantly run organization with a spectacular record of growth. Its stock may sell very high in relation to its earnings. In recent years some stocks have sold for 50 or even 100 times earnings. You may not be familiar with this phrase, so let's pause to look at it. If a company earns one dollar a share and its stock sells for 100, then it is selling for 100 times earnings. If the stock sells for 10, it is selling for 10 times earnings. Many years ago there was a well-established tradition that a stock ought to sell for 10 times what it was earning that year. That wasn't a law or a definite inviolable rule of custom but apparently it was the usual thing. But now there is no general rule—some stocks sell for 50 times, others for 20, others for 10, some for 5. Stock-market commentators try to find a reason, they develop theories to explain the differences. None of these theories will really stand the test of critical examination, but no one can deny that for years on end different types of stocks sell at different p/e (price-to-earnings) ratios whether there is a good reason or not.

Now if Company B is lucky enough to be a high p/e type, it can offer Company A $10,000,000 of its stock—it can afford to do this because its stock is selling so high. Let's suppose its stock is earning one dollar a share and selling at 50 times earnings, it would take only 200,000 shares to equal $10,000,-000 in market value. Since the company is earning only one dollar a share after taxes, it will require only $200,000 more earnings after taxes (or $400,000 before taxes) to balance the issuance of 200,000 shares to Company A.

The company has 2,500,000 shares outstanding and is earning $2,500,000 after taxes, as noted, so on a long-term basis the management is naturally confident that it can earn an additional $200,000 a year. In the meanwhile, it knows it can save $10,000,000 from the tax collector in four years or less because of the $10,000,000 tax loss of Company A. Since it has to issue 200,000 shares to do this, it is paying something for the saving. No one can really tell how much. If its earnings shoot up very rapidly it might save the whole $10,000,000 in a year or two. It is true that it now has 200,000 more shares permanently outstanding, but if it did not ever earn more or less than one dollar a share, it would be 50 years before its theoretical obligations to the new stockholders cost as much as it saved in four years or less. In the meanwhile, it had the use of the $10,000,000 saved. Now it only has to earn 2 per cent after taxes on this $10,000,000 to equal the $200,000 which has to be earned on the new shares to justify the deal.

For reasons like this Company B can offer the stockholders of Company A the full value of their loss, not in money but in stock. This stock may eventually be worth a lot more than $10,000,000. A lot of people forget that in a capitalist economy there are two types of money—government money and stock market money—and very often stock market money is the better.

There are many refinements and complications of this basic situation. One of its most significant aspects to a student of security analysis is that it illustrates the business fact that book values and real values are very different things. What is real value? Who can accurately define it? The stock market tries to reflect real value, the real value of plants, inventories, managements, products, future developments, etc. It changes its mind constantly; it never is sure and it cannot be sure.

But to get back to book value. Book value represents an effort by accountants to make an estimate of the true value of the tangible assets of a company at the end of every accounting period. It is much more defined than the constantly changing efforts of the stock market but it is not necessarily more precise. In recent years even accountants have begun to realize that their efforts are rather futile. In the now remote past before the time of World War II, accountants took their efforts at evaluation seriously. They thought that the discrepancy between an accountant's appraisal of value and the true business value of a company's assets could be kept within reasonable limits. But with the coming of World War II the philosophy of accountants had to give way to the grim facts of life.

Modern accounting represents more than anything else a skillful game played by the accountants of industry against the accountants of the Bureau of Internal Revenue. "Lifo" (last-in, first-out) methods of accounting for the value of inventory and "fast write-offs" of plant mean that the book value of a well-run company is substantially less than its replacement value and probably less than its true business value. As I mentioned earlier, the high rate of taxation also stimulates the type of accounting which minimizes the assets of a company and therefore creates a fictional low book value. Suppose you have a machine run by an expensive motor and the motor goes bad. If you buy a new motor you may have to include its cost in the value of your plant and then gradually depreciate it over a period of years according to your established depreciation schedule. But if you can put some vital new parts into the shell of the old motor, such as a new armature or brushes, then you can say these are repairs and therefore call them an operating expense rather than a capital addition to your plant. Uncle Sam will pay 52 per cent of this expense immediately. The full cost of the repair may have been just as much as a brand-new motor and the repaired motor may last just as long and do just as much work. But since it was charged off as an expense, this improvement will never show up as a greater value on the books. If you had bought a new motor, it would have shown up as an increase in your book value.

During the emergency period of World War II and the Korean War, many companies were allowed to write off new plants in five years, either fully or in large part. This was done to encourage them to build facilities which were considered vital to the national safety. Some of these companies were paying heavy excess-profit taxes. They bought new steel mills, chemical plants, electric plants, etc., and wrote them off in five years. The usual effective life of such plants may be about 20 years. But since they were written off in five, they no longer are on the books. Therefore if you look at a recent balance sheet of such a company, you may see no reflection of a large investment in modern plant and equipment which may have been made only a few years ago. You'd have to study the records intensively to get any idea of what the company really has.

Because accounting tends to confuse at least as much as it clarifies, investors very frequently lose track of all that a large company possesses. The price of the stock may grossly underestimate the true value of the company for years on end. A recent example was Crowell-Collier. Crowell-Collier owned a failing magazine, *Collier's,* and a fast-selling encyclopedia. The magazine lost what the encyclopedia made and the stock went down. New interests took charge of the company and they folded the magazine. It then became apparent that the encyclopedia was a tremendous asset which had been forgotten by investors when the magazine was alive. A few years after the magazine was buried the investors in Crowell-Collier were enjoying record prosperity.

A bigger example is the moving picture industry. Years ago the industry was dominated by giant integrated companies which owned both the studios and the theaters. The independents had a rough time because the integrated companies owned many of the best theaters. The government forced the giants to split their theaters from their studios. In recent years these theaters have become extremely valuable not as theaters but as real estate holdings. Many of them have been torn down and the land used for office buildings, hotels, and apartments. Assets which were pretty much ignored 20-odd years ago proved to be among the most valuable the companies had.

So when you glance at a balance sheet, you have to remember that there is a great deal you won't see immediately. It requires considerable labor in a financial library to reconstruct the true current value of company plants and inventories. But even this labor won't always help too much. The changing value of the dollar and the rapid pace of technological improvement have made it almost impossible for anyone to say what the true value of equipment is.

To go back to the case of Sharon Steel, the books show that it has a big investment in a 24-inch rolling mill. This is a good mill which makes what is called rolled edge strip. Strip is the name given to relatively narrow widths of thin, flat, rolled steel. When the width is greater, they are called sheets. Years ago strip had to be rolled on narrow mills, sheet on wide. But then ways were found to slit the sheets into strips. Strip that is slit from large sheets is considerably lower cost than strip that is rolled on a narrow mill. The reason for this is that it takes just about as much labor—directly and indirectly—to service a narrow mill as a wide one. Since a wide mill can handle more tons per hour, the cost per ton is lower, and so if you slit this lower-cost sheet into strips, you get a cheaper product than if you roll it on special mills. At one time it was thought that customers preferred the specially processed narrow steel, but many of the customers found that the double rolled edge which they got on the narrow mills was not significantly better. Consequently, the Sharon mill, while good mechanically, became obsolete. On the books the value of these mills looks much bigger than it is in reality. However, even this reality is somewhat uncertain. It is certain that no steel mill in any of the major industrial countries would order a new 24-inch strip mill, but it is possible that a less industrialized country could find a good use for this old mill at a secondhand price. This might be even above its present value on Sharon's books.

Thus this $72 a share book value for Sharon Steel, which

makes the stock look cheap at $40, may in some ways be an overstatement of the true value. And it may be modest in other ways. If one went through the Sharon plant and were expert enough to assign a true value to each piece of equipment, one might come up with an intelligent answer of the true current value. There can be no doubt that some of the pieces would be worth more than they are on the books, and others less. But even such an analysis would be forced to ignore certain variables which change the effective values from year to year.

For instance, Sharon has two electric furnaces at one of its plants which as electric furnaces could be rated by an expert. And he could say that they are either obsolete, reasonably modern, or excellent. But there is another problem. These furnaces are no longer located in the factory of a furnace manufacturer, ready for shipment to some steel mill. For years they have been placed in the Lowellville Works of the Sharon Steel Corporation. They were put there for a number of practical reasons, which were good at the time. Unfortunately though, the location is basically not a good one even though it was the best location at the time. As the years passed, the reasons which made it a poor location became more important and the reasons which led to the original decision became less significant. Thus the real value of equipment is not merely a coefficient of its own characteristics, factors such as its size, its age, its particular design, but also where it is being put to use. Since furnaces cannot easily be removed and reinstalled at some other location, the factor of location is an important element in their real value. All industry faces this situation. There is a constant shift in the value of its assets, due not just to general changes but to a wide variety of particular changes which affect the usefulness of the asset.

Moreover, pieces of equipment which, because of location or technological change, are not as good as the books suggest do not have a set deficiency of value. Their value as equipment changes radically, depending on the general conditions in the industry. When demand for steel is high and plants with better equipment or better locations are working at capacity, then Sharon's marginal equipment becomes very useful because Sharon can get the volume of orders that it needs to enable it to earn a good profit despite its various deficiencies. The mills which have very little value if the industry operates at 50 per cent of capacity have a substantial value, as shown by the company's earning power, when the industry operates at 80 per cent of capacity.

Table III.

SHARON STEEL CORPORATION
INCOME STATISTICS
(Million $)

Year Ended Dec. 31	Net Sales	Depreciation	Net Income
1958	99.59	3.68	0.22
1957	150.36	4.04	4.05
1956	178.68	4.07	6.91
1955	171.18	4.71	7.99
1954	98.22	3.97	3.13

In the five years from 1954–58 inclusive, Sharon earned $42,000,000 before depreciation but after taxes. This equals $40 a share for the stock. 1954 and 1958 were each recession years for the industry, so it earned most of this during the three years 1955–57 inclusive. Despite serious faults, the obsolete, badly located equipment of the company has truly large earning power under the right conditions. The obsolescence of the equipment is not an absolute measurable condition; its significance changes with the demand for the product it makes.

The same is true of good equipment: during a long industrial recession such as we had between 1930 and 1940 and which most people only dimly remember by now or never experienced, the best plants stood partly idle and therefore had low earning capacity. Since these had only recently been installed and since this installation had cost a lot of money, they were not, in some cases, even earning their depreciation charges. Labor was cheap and under such conditions old plants which had long ago been depreciated were earning as well or better than new plants. In certain cases, a new, efficient plant is no better than an old and inefficient plant unless it is working at high capacity. If labor is cheap, there isn't much dollar sense in investing in better equipment to save labor, and if demand is slack, there is no sense putting money in a high-capacity machine when you can't sell the tons of material it can turn out.

During these slack times professional investors paid very little attention to the value of plant and equipment. When companies were sold, the plant and equipment were often thrown in free; the buyer would pay only for the quick assets such as easily sold inventory, easily collected accounts receivable. For a number of years the real worth of many fine companies was well below their book values. Then there came a time when business was better but not yet booming, and the stock markets were still uncertain of the future, when the real value was above the book values but the stock values were lower. This was a harvest time for sharpshooters who understood intellectually or instinctively the value theory of security analysis. That was followed by a time of generally high economic activity when the real value of good equipment, as well as good sales organizations, good research departments, etc., was generally much greater than the book values and when the market reflected this in stock values which were clearly higher than the book values and might or might not be higher than the indefinable true values, which are produced partly by the times themselves. To appraise book value, then, the investor must make some sort of appraisal of the general economic future.

By now I have made you realize that no matter how many courses you take on security analysis, you cannot turn to a company's books and get a neat, accurate idea of what the value of its stock should be. The fact that a stock is selling for less than its book value is not by itself a significant clue to an unusually cheap stock. Nor does the fact that many stocks sell for far more than their book values mean that they are grossly overpriced. There is no certainty of any sort as to what the book value really means, nor is there a way to get at a true value in a clear, scientific way. A business judgment must always be made and thus security analysis must always in the end enter into the mystery of an art.

But while there is no certainty as to what book value signifies, it would be going to an extreme to say that it had no significance at all. When you have a high book value, you at least can feel sure that the company has a lot of assets of some sort to work with. You don't know what they are really worth but you can feel sure that when you visit the plant you will have something to look at. Actually, in Sharon's case, it is obvious that there is a substantial value of some sort there. The simple fact that it made a lot of money in a five-year period, one which included two recessions, shows that the book value is not at all an insignificant guide in true worth.

If you visited the management, you would, in this case, begin to see that there are things which can be done with the plant to make the book value closer to real value, and you would learn that some things have been done and others are in the process of being done. As is the case with any company management, their decisions can radically alter the prospects of a company. There is nothing set or static about any company, and therefore the thing that is significant about book value or the individual items of the balance sheet which contribute to book value is the clue that it gives to the various things which a management might do or may have to do.

When an analyst sees that a stock is selling at a low or reasonable price in relation to the values which he finds indicated in the balance, he has a clue to, rather than a proof of, what may be an unusually good opportunity. His next questions are whether the management can do something unusual with the assets it has, whether it has a plan to do this, etc.

The management of Sharon Steel is thoroughly cognizant of the defects of the company and also of what has to be done to change the situation. It may be worthwhile for the student to look into their minds to gain a general understanding of how the destinies of companies are changed.

Sharon has a number of faults, the most crucial of which is that it is limited by the width of its narrow rolling mills in the range of products it can offer customers. This has a number of undesirable effects. One has already been mentioned—companies owning wider mills can offer the same products at lower prices. But this is not only the question of slitting wide sheets into narrow strips. To understand Sharon's problems the reader must understand a little bit about basic industrial functioning—whether it is the function of a steel mill, a flour mill, an aluminum plant, or a chemical plant.

The basic situation is this: equipment costs money. The equipment must pay back the money by producing material or services. If a plant can be kept busy, then the unit cost of the through-put is lower than if it cannot operate steadily. Thus steel companies with wide mills can sell wide products to some customers and narrow ones to others and keep their mills busy continuously—or fairly so—while Sharon, having narrow mills, is limited to customers who need narrow products. When times are slack, Sharon cannot find enough customers to keep its mills busy. The companies with wide mills may, because they serve a wider variety of customer needs; therefore if they fill up their mills, their costs per ton of strip are lower. Sharon must sell at the same price as the big mill competitors or it would get no business at all. When times are slack, its profits drop even faster than its sales. When times are good, the owners of large mills aren't so anxious for narrow-strip business to fill their mill schedules and there is a big demand for strip anyway. Under those conditions, Sharon's costs become good even though it has narrow mills because the mills are fully occupied. It is not the width of the mill which makes Sharon's costs bad so much as the conditions of the market. This is the reason that Sharon does earn very good money in good times and this is the reason why its plant is valuable despite its faults.

Sharon has virtues. The main one is that it has a lot of capacity in relation to the cost of its plant. Sharon can make about 1,000,000 tons of finished steel products of various types, and if there is demand for all it can make, its sales can total about $200,000,000. Its plant has a book value of only about $40,000,000. A new plant of this capacity could not possibly be built for $40,000,000. If it were built entirely new, it would probably cost $300,000,000. If this new plant has the same capacity of finished products as the present plant, this would mean a capital cost of $300 a ton of capacity. If this were amortized over a ten-year period, it would be necessary to charge $30 depreciation for every ton produced over a ten-year period if the average operating rate during that period were 100 per cent. If the average rate were 75 per cent, which is much more likely, then $40 a ton would have to be charged to depreciation. If the amortizing period were 15 years and the average operating rate were 75 per cent, the charge per ton per year on account of depreciation would be $26.65, and if it were a 20-year schedule, the average charge per ton would be about $20.

In the case of actual plant, which has a book value of only $40,000,000, the average charge per ton for ten years at a 75-per-cent rate is only $5.35, for 15 years only $3.25, and for 20 years only $2.65. Thus while the old plant has the vices of inefficiency, it has the virtue of costing very little. If the demand for steel is big enough to make operations profitable, very little of the profits are needed to pay back the cost of the plant. (It should be noted that if a company has built a new plant with its own money, the pay-back of this cost is to its own treasury and the cost of this repayment is to some extent a bookkeeping concept, but if it has raised money from the public either by borrowing money or selling stock, the need to earn the cost of the plant is a very real one. The clarity of this real need is clearer in the case where the money is borrowed and has to be repaid than in the case where new stock was sold. But it is a real cost in either case because unless the new plant pays for itself the management was foolish to raise new money. It was also foolish to use its own money—in other words, foolishness has its A, B, C grades.)

Let's take one part of Sharon's plant as an example: it has a bank of old open-hearth furnaces which can melt at

the rate of 15-17 tons of steel per hour. A new oxygen con-
verter furnace can melt steel at the rate of 90 to 110 tons
per hour. It takes about the same number of men directly
to operate the old and the new furnaces and just the same
number of bookkeepers, stenographers, company officers,
etc., to supervise them. Thus the operating costs of new
furnaces per ton of steel melted are much lower than of the
old. Since the new furnace can turn out six or seven times as
much per melt, it follows that the labor and overhead per
ton are only one-sixth or one-seventh that of the old furnaces. But it costs money to build new furnaces. Each ton of
steel melted must bear part of this cost until the furnace is
paid for or, as accountants say, depreciated.

Now if these old furnaces have been written off, then
there is no depreciation to charge. The low cost or lack of
depreciation can go a long way to balance the high cost of
operation. Sharon has been unlucky having its old furnaces,
but also technological change has finally brought it some
good luck—in the last few years it has become possible for a
steel company to modernize its furnace capacity at a much
lower capital cost than formerly. The new oxygen processes
have opened up possibilities which were not available ten
years ago. For about $20,000,000 the company can have a
complete new furnace set-up. If written off in five years, this
would add only four dollars a ton to the cost of melting
during those years and this would be paid for by savings in
labor costs. After the write-off, Sharon would make a profit
on its investment. If Sharon had modernized some years ago,
it might have chosen to use old and more expensive techniques. By waiting it failed to make as much as it might have
in years past but it had the luck to benefit from the advance
in technology.

In 1955 the management made the first move toward the curing of Sharon's problem by authorizing the purchase of a new blooming mill. The mill, costing $14,000,000, was put into operation early in 1957. A blooming mill is the primary mill of a steel plant. The width of the blooming mill, the power of the machinery driving its rollers, the speed at which it operates are key facts determining the total capacity and also the variety of products produced by the entire mill it serves. The new bloomer made it possible to roll more stainless as well as wider slabs of ordinary steel. It was put in the main works, a large plant with plenty of good flat land surrounding it, and it was placed so that when the company is able to build a new, wide, hot sheet mill, it can extend out from where the bloomer is now located and the new mill can be built without interrupting the functioning of the old.

When the new hot sheet mill is installed, Sharon will also have to add some type of new cold mill. There are several types. This, however, is not a major job.

With the addition of the new mills, Sharon will become a grade B instead of a grade D operation. Its major difficulties will then be over. It has other problems. Its blast furnaces will never have the lowest costs because they have medium capacities and in this business high volume and low costs are almost always synonymous. But its iron costs can be brought down substantially by building an ore sintering plant or by extensive use of pellet ore and by using oxygen in its blast furnaces as well as in the new oxygen steel-making furnaces.

All this improvement, of course, will cost money. One of the most important questions facing the security analyst who has looked at Sharon and understands its industrial problems and possibilities is—how will the money be raised? This is where analysis of the financial figures, of the balance sheet and the income account becomes important. How much money has the company now? How much could be raised by some readjustment of accounts (for example, by letting inventories run down, by cutting maintenance for a while)? What might be the repercussions of this? What is the cash flow history of the company (cash flow is the combination of cash flowing into the company treasury from depreciation charges and of earnings after taxes)? What is the present debt of the company and how soon does it have to be paid off? If it is being paid off in installments, how big are these and would it be wise to try to change them? This might be done by refinancing the present debt. How much more debt could the company carry? The answer to this depends in part on the estimated effect of the plant improvement program under good conditions and bad. If a very large part of the money needed for the mill is raised by selling more stock to the public or by selling convertible bonds or preferred stocks which are convertible into stock at a low price, then Sharon is a much less interesting speculation than if the company can generate a good deal of the cash needed from its own operations and borrow the rest.

During the five years 1961–65 inclusive it should, even if some of the years are poor, be able to earn and keep after dividends a substantial part of what is needed to improve its plant. But since the total program may cost not far from $100,000,000, it will probably have to borrow $50,000,000. If money were plentiful, it would have no problem, but because of the hard-money policy of the government and for other reasons money was tight in the last years of the 1950–59 decade and at the start of the 1960's. Sharon probably cannot raise what it needs on a straight bond; it will have to sell some convertibles or some stock. Since its 1,100,-000 shares of common stock are selling for only $40,000,000 to $50,000,000 in the market, it would have to sell over 1,000,000 shares to raise $50,000,000, which would be impossible under existing conditions. It wouldn't be practical to double the number of shares and sell another 1,000,000 at $40 a share; they would have to be sold for less than the present market which would make matters still worse. It would be possible to sell $50,000,000 in convertibles if the bonds were convertible at 40 or even 50, but this also would mean that eventually there would be over 2,000,000 shares outstanding. Even though the new equipment will make Sharon a much more efficient company and even though it might earn at least twice as much as it has, the present shareholder might not benefit much if these doubled earnings had to be divided among twice as many shares of stock. This sort of thing is called dilution.

The problem of analyzing Sharon is, therefore, not a simple one. What we have finally arrived at is an understanding that the company has a genuine potential for money making which, if the management is fortunate and clever in its financing, can be exploited so that the stock turns out to be an unusually good investment. I think an analyst would feel that it is a stock worth taking some chance on. The fact that it has collected over $40,000,000 in cash from depreciation and earnings after taxes in five confused years will reassure him, since this about equals the total current market valuation of the stock. But he has to remain uncertain as to just how good he thinks it is. He must become aware that the book-value figure, the enticing suggestion that the stock ought to sell for about double what it is selling at, has some of the siren's false lure. Maybe Sharon's management can make an honest woman out of this beautiful beckoning book value. That is what book values always are: a suggestion, not a certainty.

CHAPTER NINE

Techniques of Security Analysis—
the Growth Concept

The other principal analytical concept is growth. To my mind it is obvious that growth is a more profound concept than value—value is deceptive as a philosophy because, as I hope I have amply illustrated, there is no way to measure value with a precision which is as real as it seems to be. Also, there is something wrong in wishing to buy lots of bargains. You can only get a bargain if for some reason the person who owns what you are buying is stupid or innocent or so badly hurt in some way that he must give it to you. Naturally if there are bargains around, there is no reason why you shouldn't take advantage of them, and since there always are some bargains, it's a good idea to know how to go about assessing them. In times of depression there are many bargains, but it has seemed to me at various times since 1932, when I heard rich men saying how they had sold out and were waiting for the next collapse of business, that it was rather cruel to hope that the country would be involved in another major economic disaster, that thousands of innocent investors would be forced to sacrifice their holdings so that you—the wise, the prudent, the thrifty, and the hard—would pick them up. Those who have year after year been waiting for another depression and have kept their funds in cash and bonds have been rewarded for what is basically an unsocial attitude—they have missed thousands of opportunities.

Growth is the big thing because growth is life. Since growth is life, it is the reason why it is possible to make a great deal of money in an investment without being particularly intelligent. I have tried to say in various ways that you don't have to be bright to be rich. I am sure that everyone my age has met rich people who were not very bright and non-rich ones who were charming and intelligent. But there are also poor people who are stupid and wealthy ones who are intelligent and sometimes even charming. It is very hard to believe that the situation is so carelessly arranged because wealth gives such power that one cannot help but think that somewhere there must be some hidden close correlation between the two forces—wealth and intelligence. The reason there isn't is that wealth, like the existence of the rich person himself, is a product of nature. Man's intelligence did not create nature, but nature created all the potential of man's wealth. We don't understand nature completely but we can accept it completely. I stress this because it is one of the hopeful things about the stock market. The market is very responsive to nature—human nature, solar nature, any sort you wish—and so you can, and many people have, become rich without any unusual use of intelligence, whether you have it or not. The way this happens is through growth. You have to be quite bright and work hard to be a really good value analyst—and I have seen the best lose quite a lot of money after a good deal of hard analysis—but you don't have to be bright to make money through growth; you can drift along with this force like the Mississippi River.

The stock market also gives us a rather unique opportunity to grow wealthier without work. Each occupation has some special quality; the stock market is no better for making money than many other businesses. It is good but that is not its unique quality. Its unique quality is the ease with which fortunes can come to you. I am sure you are not going to agree with this, so let's look at the case of two cousins, each of whom I have known many years.

Cousin Mustard started with nothing and worked hard and did very well; recently he told me he was worth a half million. Besides that he stands very high in his profession, and rightly so, as he is as sharp and savory as mustard. One day Cousin Frank Hamburger came to him for advice. Mustard called me up the next morning: "What do you think Frank is worth—one million dollars—can you beat that? I saw his list—the best—Standard of New Jersey, Telephone, Du Pont, I.B.M., a million easily." I could understand Mustard's feeling since I had known the cousins so long. Frank never worked an effective week in his life. He tried—he wasn't lazy—nothing would have made him happier than to have been able to earn his living, but he was the sort who couldn't have been a garbage collector because he would have forgotten to collect it. He started with a reasonable amount of capital—maybe $100,000—and he lived on his income and, lo and behold, today he is worth an easy $1,000,000.

Of course you can see your fortune shrink away quietly also. Forty years ago—and this is not really a long time— everyone thought that if you owned enough stock in some of the great railroads, you wouldn't have to worry much about the future—"Put 'em away and forget 'em"—but there has been a tremendous shrinkage of fortune over this extended period among major owners of rail stocks because the industry has gone downhill. I do not wish to imply that in the market you can make a fortune easily and also with complete safety.

Safety for the typical investor can only be had by diversification. An individual business is a remarkably fragile plant, but like many fragile plants it also has remarkable vitality. It is subject therefore to sudden changes. It takes fairly constant watching of a well-informed sort to keep track of a large investment in a single company. If you know a company well, if you have a very close connection with the management (through friendship, parentage, or marriage— something really close), and if you are a cool-headed, realistic person, you can do very well by keeping your eggs in one basket. If you diversify, you will almost certainly do less well than if you concentrate and are fortunate, but real concentration cannot be advised as a public policy.

As a personal policy I follow a policy of concentration. For instance, at one time about one-third of my family funds were invested in American Telephone and another 40 per cent in Air Products, High Voltage Engineering, Stauffer Chemical, and Puerto Rico Telephone. I give you these specific names because it seems to me that the expert should show what he really does. I feel that as a person who is asking for public attention I am just like a ballplayer or a boxer—I have to swing at something. You may think—American Telephone is a hell of a stock for a wizard of Wall Street to put one-third of his money in. I could tell from the glazed look in my customers' eyes that they thought this was a dull stock for me to tell them to buy. It seemed to me that it had a unique combination of essential safety with very marked growth possibilities. I said this as strongly as I could in a series of recommendations, and at the end of 1960 I had the remarkable experience of not only enjoying a large capital gain but also of being for one week a sort of Wall Street hero because I had recommended Telephone so strongly. This was partly a matter of luck. A few weeks before the year's end I had said in my Letter that Telephone would raise its dividend to $3.60 before its next annual meeting which was in May, 1961. Two weeks later the management announced that they would increase the dividend to $3.60—just as I had said—and make the first payment at the new rate in July, 1961. I didn't get this from the management but few believed me. I got it from an old friend of mine, Ted Locke, who is one of the best analysts of public utilities that Wall Street has had. He knew a lot more about the company than I and he had been recommending Telephone for a long while also, but I am a writer and I invent expressive phrases and so more people know what I think. And I had been raving about Telephone for almost two years. People love to chatter and so I thought that all the telephone companies would continue to grow. New means of chatter have been opened up by computers and various sorts of modern data-processing equipment and this means that businessmen could soon chatter in an endless, enthusiastic detailed way about business the way women do about love, dress, and family, and at the same time new electronic devices have or will so cheapen the cost of long-distance chatter that women will be able to do what businessmen long have been doing, chatter over thousands of miles without thinking too much of the cost. I didn't like Telephone just because it was so sound, so strong, so old. I loved it because I thought communication was one of the great pleasures of life and therefore chatter was one of the great growth industries of the future.

A growth stock doesn't have to be something daring and reckless. Strong, old, big companies can grow too, and you can increase your fortune very substantially by investing in a very large company during a dynamic period of its history. I concentrated in Du Pont in 1953 for the same philosophic reasons that I concentrated in Telephone in 1959. Sharpshooting investors also had a glazed look in their eyes then —Du Pont was too safe. But by 1955 it was selling almost three times as high. Of course there were stocks which did better than that but not with such a safety factor. For some people safety—because of various personal reasons—is much less important than for others. For me safety is important— and making money has been important too—so I have always tried to work out combinations which are satisfactory to me. No doubt by some people's standards I have failed to be adequately daring—by others I have been breathlessly reckless. So far as I am concerned, I feel I have achieved my objective. Two of the other companies mentioned above—High Voltage Engineering and Air Products—you probably have never heard of. Concentrating substantial sums in them represents a degree of daring which can only be justified—logically—if one is professional. While I believe in concentration for professionals or for those who have the very highest professional guidance, the more I see of what goes on in actual business, the more I realize that the only way most investors can achieve a high degree of safety is through a considerable amount of diversification.

You may understand this if I tell you a bit of what happened to my Air Products. I started buying this stock at 25 in 1958 and I bought it as high as 64 in 1959. Then at one time in 1960 it was as low as 29—but then climbed back, and recently stood at about 50. It is obvious that when the stock was 29, late in 1960, it represented a very poor investment. Not only did I have a huge loss on the $64 stock; all the profit I once had had on the low-priced purchase also disappeared. My customers were patient with me but they weren't pleased. How did this happen? It is probably too complicated a story to tell here. For one thing I obviously became too enthusiastic—the very large volume of business being done by Air Products, the much larger volume which would clearly be done in the future because of the new plants the company was building and whose production was contracted for, the very interesting possibilities of new developments in the company's chosen area of competence—cryogenics (i.e., very-low-temperature reactions), its extremely distinguished technical record, all these made me feel this was a most unusual stock. And I still think it is—I am holding it and believe I'll do well in the end. But I overlooked some things, some of which I perhaps couldn't help but overlook, others which I might have caught had I not fallen in love with the situation.

Some were as seemingly minor as the fact that the president's car wouldn't start when he took us to the country club for lunch. Its battery was dead. I couldn't see how this was allowed to happen. There were other larger and clearer questions too—more typical of security analysis. For instance, I was told that earnings would not be so good that year, that the stockholder would have to wait until the new plants came in and were operating and until the extra expense associated with building the new plants was a thing of the past. I felt that the market would think this was nothing but a temporary delay in the development of larger earnings and would have confidence in the company's future growth and therefore continue to give the stock a high valuation. The trouble really was that for a variety of reasons, never entirely clear to me, the market began to develop an increasing lack of confidence in the company's future. I had complete confidence in the management, and the market's lack of confidence puzzled me—like someone not liking a girl that I liked. Impatient investors began to be skeptical of the management's capabilities. Earnings were worse than I and others had been led to believe. Numerous stories circulated that the company had been forced by competition to take some major contracts at too low a price (the company did have a bad experience with certain contracts) and this was never clearly explained. Officers of steel companies who gave Air Products contracts for the new plants admired the equipment but said they could not see how Air Products hoped to make much money out of the contract. A great many people began to have their doubts and toward the end of 1960, just when better earnings were about to become evident, the stock collapsed to a level which was hardly higher than it had been three years before at the depth of the 1957–58 recession.

Concentration can be gloriously profitable but it also can be extremely dangerous—even when you make a very substantial effort to know all the facts—because there are forces within you—cupidity, exaggerated hopes, emotional feelings of friendship, failure to know of something better to do with your money, etc.—which can sway your judgment. This can happen even though you know it's happening; these psychological forces can be like physical forces—you know they are operating but you can't get out of their grip. Even if you are basically right in your analysis, other people can reach a wrong conclusion whose effect is temporarily more powerful than the right conclusion you have reached. If you have concentrated in a situation which is being depressed by the skepticism of many powerful investors, you will lose money and you will also lose the opportunity to invest in something else. And if you have borrowed heavily to make the investment you can be sold out. This sometimes happens in a sad way just before the turn comes.

The tactic of concentration can be modified by concentrating in an industry rather than a company. This is frequently done by professionals. For example, it may be impossible to tell which is the best maker of solid-state devices, but there was no doubt a few years ago that such devices were in for big growth, so profitable concentration in this growth area without undue risk could be achieved by buying stocks of a half dozen makers of transistors or diodes. But an investor following this sensible pattern of diversificacation would almost inevitably have dissipated some of his profit possibilities. For instance, he probably would have put some money in General Transistor (a company which did spectacularly well for a while but faded in the race), and he probably would have been intrigued by transistor developments at Philco—certainly he could have found very high-level technicians of independent judgment who thought the world of the Philco transistor. There would have been moments when he thought the bird had flown from the bush into his hands. But the bird flew away again—Philco's stock ended in 1960 at half the price it started.

One of the problems in successfully investing in growth companies which are also science companies is to find those which really are technical leaders. The difficulty lies in this: if you could hire a highly qualified technician to tell you which was good and which not so good, this would mean that the question was so simple that all the companies involved in a certain scientific area would have the same good technique. Qualified technicians can save you from egregious error. I use technical back-up liberally, but I recognize that some of the problem is beyond such a simple solution. Therefore the man you want to hire really doesn't exist. In a long-established industry such as steel, aluminum, etc., there is very little difference between techniques other than the age of the plants. Therefore when you analyze companies in such industries you are making more of an economic analysis than a technical analysis. For instance, if the demand for steel improves sharply in 1961–62 over 1960–61 then Sharon Steel which has a class D plant will be as good and maybe a little better speculative investment than U.S. Steel which has spent billions on modernization. But in a rapidly developing new industry, technique can be all-important. Fairchild Camera, which acquired a solid states transistor diode group by merger, proved to be one of the outstanding money-making stocks of the 1958–60 stretch while Raytheon which made the first transistors was just as dismal a stock to buy as any dull old steel stock. It didn't look that way for a while but it turned out that way. So you cannot sort it out just by following the sound procedure of hiring qualified advisors, and in the case of a new technique there are in a certain sense no known qualified advisors: one group of technicians follows one line of development; another, another; each so far as you can tell are qualified scientists, but the road divides and one leads to much better things than the other. Which group you follow depends therefore on a mystery element—call it luck, call it an intuitive capability of understanding the right people and therefore somehow picking those who prove to be the brightest, flatter yourself or be modest, whichever it is; the fact is that there remains a certain amount of mystery about profits or losses.

So you should not be discouraged. For the person who understands that there is a problem which no system can eliminate and who has honestly calculated the risk I advise trying to concentrate in a few growth situations. If he really is very daring I would always pick small ones (but this phrase "really daring" has a false ring of heroism about it— the object of investing is not being a hero but to make money). If you find something which is very speculative but which gives you somehow a very honest feeling of a very unusual opportunity then I would take a chance. If you have an honest sense of daring—the sort you are scarcely conscious of and which does not give you the vain feeling of being a hero—then I would not restrain it, but I would always strive to have an honest feeling. It can be very dangerous to force your feelings because this is the way you kid yourself. If you are in doubt, it may be worth remembering that I had an argument with a very gifted analyst at a Christmas party in 1958. I had just sold a small amount of Ampex I owned—he was buying more. I told him I was buying Telephone. When Christmas of 1960 came around, Ampex, despite the marvelous newness of videotape and all the wonderful ultra new things in its laboratories, was selling for 40 per cent less than when I sold it, while Telephone, despite the simple familarity of its main product and the disgusting, dull safety of the investment, was selling for 40 per cent more. And how about High Voltage, another stock I mentioned owning? In late 1960 that was selling for 100 per cent more than in December, 1958, and 500 per cent more than when I bought it in panicky 1957. I would have been even better off if I had put the money I put into Telephone into High Voltage but it would have been a much bigger risk. I had been honest with myself—I took the risks I really wanted to take and left heroism (and disasters I have at times seen go with it) to others.

Do I know any heroes who didn't meet disaster? The people I have known long enough to feel sure that they really have been extremely successful in Wall Street have heroic qualities but they also have cautious qualities. Most of them have been professionals, therefore they had a business to carry them along when their speculations weren't working smoothly. They all gave their full time to investing and developed substantial sources of information. They all, of course, gained experience over the years and learned from their mistakes. If you analyzed their deeds and daring against their total background I think you would find that while they truly dared they were never suicidal.

Despite these reservations—the reality of which I have learned from experience—I continue to hire qualified technical advisors. If I did not, I would be completely lost when it came to judging technical industries. While I may miss the best despite the best efforts and even pick the mediocre, I feel sure that with good advice I am very unlikely to make an absurd choice. I must say that while I have missed some good opportunities I have had rather good luck in those selections I have made. If you meet enough technical people you begin to get some idea of what realities in the area are, and then you have to form a human judgment: is the man you are talking to for real or is he somehow not for real? I try to combine technical advice with an intuitive appraisal of human qualities.

There are no growth trends—there are growth openings. Some managements open big new opportunities in the vast mysterious thing that is nature, others open small; some managements are timid and don't take advantage of these openings, some are reckless, some are dishonest, some are bold and able. The truth is there are no real trends, not only in securities or in business but in anything else. There are developments but not trends. When a development—either one or a series of them—has a profound effect which lasts for generations, practical statisticians call this a trend.

You can clarify the trend problem for yourself by getting the statistics on corn production from the U.S. Department of Agriculture and plotting it on graph paper. You can then draw a trend line through the series of dots made by putting the data on the paper. It will become obvious that if you draw the line backward far enough it will go to the other side of the axis of the data and show that at that time no corn was produced in the United States. You can check the time at which the trend line crosses the axis and you'll see that this was not historically correct. Corn was grown in America at that time. Now if you draw the trend line forward far enough you'll see that at some time in the future the weight of all the corn grown in the U.S.A. will equal the weight of the earth itself. In other words, trend lines always lead to absurd conclusions if they are extended far enough. Trend lines are only useful within a limited time span. This is because there are no real trends—there are events some of which are very extended and some of which are brief. For most businesses events are quite brief. There are very few really extended growth trends based on a reasonably regular annual rate of increase. The utility industry has had a strong and regular trend of growth for many years. The Telephone Company has had a 7-per-cent annually compounded growth trend of revenues for about 15 years. Du Pont once had an 18-per-cent growth trend for about 15 years, but most so-called growth trends in business are nothing but extended periods of expansion due to some very special and definite development in products and/or techniques.

The growth-trend theory of investment can be used as a gimmick for sales promotion or a rationalization of a dramatic industrial development which has been going on and seemingly won't stop soon. But it will stop after a while and most trends stop much quicker than speculators expect them to when they are moved by a moment of passionate avarice. You should really be very careful not to take formulas for evaluating growth stocks too seriously. If promoters are working in a stock and using such a formula as a gimmick, try to take advantage of what they are doing and sell out before they stop talking or before the growth ends. Try to analyze what force is behind the growth and what is causing a pattern which looks like a trend but really is just an extended development. Of course not all promoters are dishonest—they promote to themselves too. They overstay the market because the trend which never was really there vanishes, and they, along with their faithful but victimized followers, are left with dreams of fortunes they might have had.

Profound effects are real and do occur with companies. A profound effect will cause a big jump in sales and earnings and in the value of the stock, but to try to reduce the concept of this effect to simple arithmetic such as a 10-per-cent growth trend, a 20 per cent, a 30 per cent, etc., is, I think, misleading. It is more misleading when one tries to discount it scientifically. For instance, if you think that a certain company earning one dollar a share now is going to earn three dollars a share ten years from now, the problem arises what should you pay for this prospect now? Let's suppose that if it were earning three dollars a share now you might pay 30, what should you pay as things stand when it is earning one dollar now and you hope (for good reasons) it earns three dollars ten years from now. Should you pay 15—20—25—what? There are many things to consider. If you think its growth will level off ten years from now, you will pay less than if you think it will keep on growing in this way and earn nine dollars a share 20 years from now. But no matter what your concept of future development is, the price you pay will represent some sort of anticipation of the future and some sort of adjustment of this anticipation for the years you have to wait. In other words, you will pay more for a stock with growing earnings than one whose earnings are stable, but you won't willingly pay as much for these future earnings now as you will ten years later when they prove out.

It is possible to make a mathematical formula out of this general problem to help decide how much it is reasonable to anticipate the future and how much you should subtract from this anticipation because the future will take some time to turn into the present. The trouble with doing this is that the formulas are bound to translate a generally correct conclusion with false precision.

The false precision is exemplified by the tables in Burton Crane's *The Sophisticated Investor*. In Chapter X, which he wrote in 1958, he makes estimates for the 1962 earnings of certain growth stocks and develops theoretical prices for them based on the formula. Here is what the formula called for and what has happened so far.

Table IV.

Estimated 1962 earnings after discounting	MRK	PRD	ROH	GLW
20	63½	51½	185½	26
15	47½	39	144	19½
Actual prices				
9/5/58	65	67½	405	92
2/20/60	80	186½	728	133½
1/15/61	80	178	653	176

The prices in the line "after discounting" represent two possibilities—one developing out of capitalizing the estimate of future earnings at 20 times that estimate and the other at 15 times and then discounting that capitalization by the chosen discount factor, which in this formula is 0.635. Each of these lines represents theoretical prices. The last three lines represent actual market prices—the top one being the prices at the time Burton wrote the chapter, the second and third being those at the time I am writing. It can be seen that actual prices have been consistently higher than the theoretical prices.

What is wrong with the formula is not the general concept that it might be useful to develop a relationship between growth if it develops as you think it will and what should be paid for that growth now; it is the precision with which you are tempted to apply the formula once you have it. Just as the value analysts erred because they were seeking a false precision—because they thought there must be some sort of way of relating true value with various accounting measures of tangible value so as to know whether stocks were over-priced or underpriced—so growth-formula analysts develop a false sense of precision out of their formulas: either they expect too much and are disappointed (as I was in the case of Air Products) when there is a change in investor confidence in a certain company—or they expect too little. While growth is extremely important, it is not the only quality investors want; growth formulas can lead to false conclusions because they overemphasize growth just as value formulas over-emphasize values. Burton says that the formula really results in nothing more than a formulized guess and that it is possible to apply the formula so that a variety of guesses is achieved.

The best exposition of growth-trend theory however is Crane's *The Sophisticated Investor.* I think putting growth into a theorem leads to over-precision but one practical thing would be to buy the book, study the formulas, get some practice with them, and see how they work. If you make money with them, they are good. When you start to lose, close the book.

Formulas for investing are, to my mind, like formulas for painting or writing or making war or doing any other thing: they can have a certain usefulness, they are at least a way to get started, but if you mistake them for the real thing, then they will lead you astray.

One of these important investment problems is age. You'll find many capable ex-businessmen sitting in brokers' offices, using the capital they made when they were vigorously in business to trade in securities. These are very able people, but they decided or their doctors told them that the hurly-burly of business was too much for them.

The practical problem of using capital to maintain the highest standards of living of wealthy men and women for years and even decades after their vitality has ebbed means that a very high premium is paid for really reliable business management. The growth factor is not the only reason why certain stocks sell at much higher prices than others in relation to their earnings. Belief that certain managements will somehow or other—by research, by intelligent mergers and acquisitions, by well-conducted sales programs and other means—find ways of solving the problems of the future, and make progress in terms of earnings and dividends which cannot be clearly estimated now, is the reason why stocks like Corning Glass and Rohm and Haas and quite a few others continue to sell high during years when there is no clear-cut indication of unusual growth.

Forgetting growth trends but accepting growth as the true and greatest reality of investing, how does one find a growing situation? Apparently this isn't too hard—people are constantly picking them. Growth stocks like Polaroid, Dow Chemical, I.B.M., Rohm and Haas, Thiokol, Texas Instruments, Du Pont, etc., are owned by tens of thousands of people. Even less-known growth stocks, like High Voltage Engineering, Air Products, Avon Products, Stauffer Chemical, Fairchild Camera, Transitron, are owned by thousands. Growth stocks are not exactly a secret to the investing public.

Wall Street has about 100,000 salesmen working on the public, and since growth stocks are popular, it would be very hard to find the one that investors haven't heard about. The real trick today is not that of being aware of the exceptional investment value of growth but to avoid paying too much for growth or of being confused between true and phony growth. I think it is very hard to turn this trick; at least it is hard to describe how to do it in a way which would convince anyone familiar with the problem.

Those who believe in growth-stock formulas have tried to answer the problem with their formulas, but as I have said, these are treacherous because growth does not go by trends but by jumps or leaps. Moreover, a growth stock does not get its value solely from demonstrable growth; it gets it a great deal from faith in the management, a belief that somehow or other the business will grow even though there is no evidence of it. For instance, in 1961 a doctor alerted me to a closed TV program which was to be put on by G. D. Searle and Company, a very fine maker of pharmaceuticals. The program, he said, would deal with Searle's remarkable hormone product Enovid. I had known about Enovid from the time it was first announced in 1957. But now things finally looked exciting. Enovid, as you also probably know by now, can be used to control ovulation. If the egg does not move into the uterus then, of course, pregnancy will not occur. It serves the dual purpose of making a woman more likely to become pregnant when she wishes and certain not to if she does not wish. But if a woman takes a suitable dose as regularly as prescribed, she won't menstruate. The control of menstruation certainly should be a great convenience for women. I didn't know all of this in 1957, when the drug was first announced, but I knew some of it.

Between 1957 and 1961 extensive testing of the drug was

conducted in Puerto Rico and other places and it was established that it worked very reliably and also produced no important undesirable side effects. Moreover, the tests indicated that it might have some anti-cancer action. This was totally unexpected. I might pause here and stress again what I may have said much too frequently, which is that there is this mystery element in all phases of investment—the Dr. Jekyll as well as the Mr. Hyde company runs into the golden as well as the icy unexpected. Whether the drug has a real anti-cancer effect remains to be seen—a five-year clinical program involving 6,000 women has been announced—so it will take some years to get a more certain idea. But the possibility that the drug could reduce breast and cervical cancer was, in my opinion, more important than its birth-control potential.

The idea that women want to have a firm, rational control over pregnancy is a man's idea. A neurotic woman becomes an old maid largely because she is afraid of sex. She is not afraid of birth but birth is the most evident confirmation of her suppressed and confused and tragic fear of sex. So she welcomes anything which would establish control over birth because she thinks that this might remove her fear of sex. But the normal woman does not fear sex or birth; she welcomes it. Birth creates a problem but a woman doesn't necessarily want to avoid problems any more than a man does. She also doesn't necessarily want to remove problems from the life of a man she admires or loves. While she wants to give pleasure she doesn't want to become a fun thing. Woman is a mystery. She appreciates that she is a mystery and she enjoys all the aspects of it—even that of denying at times that she is a mystery. Women do, of course, use contraceptive devices. The trouble with the Searle's pill—it seemed to me —wasn't that it was contraceptive but that it had to be taken regularly. The woman has to swallow a pill 20 days every month—she might miss a day now and then but failure to be systematic about it would negate the whole thing. I didn't think women would be that systematic about avoiding pregnancy, and the drug had been no great sales success even though doctors knew about it since 1957. The table below shows that Searle's earnings enjoyed nothing more than a mild and halting rise from 1955 through the first nine months of 1960. But when I learned that it might have anti-cancer action I felt differently. Women have a deep fear of breast cancer, not only because of the danger but because of the maiming effects of the cure. The loss of a breast—one of the great psychological compensations for the subconscious belief that she has lost a once-possessed penis—is a blow beyond that of the physical damage done and danger faced. I feel sure that if it is proved that Enovid substantially reduces the incidence of breast cancer and if the drug is reduced sufficiently in price, women will take it regularly for that reason. Their mystery will be preserved and their beauty defended.

Table V.
G. D. SEARLES
EARNINGS AND PRICE RANGE

Year	Net Per Share	Price Range	
		H	L
1960 (9 mos.)	$1.26	70	52
1959	1.65	58	45
1958	1.58	58	38
1957	1.58	55	35
1956	1.50	53	34
1955	1.40	37	28

All this was and remains pure speculation. What wasn't speculation and what made the stock shoot up suddenly to new all-time highs was the virtual certainty that the *Reader's Digest* would have a big story about Enovid. Everyone in Wall Street remembers what the *Reader's Digest* did for Kent cigarettes and therefore for Lorillard, the company which makes Kents—and a big blast written with the typical nice, naïve, and honest enthusiasm of the *Reader's Digest* I felt would do wonders for the stock. So when my informant who was an editor of a medical magazine told me about the *Digest* article, I bought stock. This was what the faithful holders of Searle's stock had been waiting for all these years —this break in which science, sales, and innocent promotion were mixed in explosive quantities. They had faith that it would happen because it happened before when Searle brought out Dramomine and Banthine. When years went by and nothing big came out of the large, indeed the ever-growing-larger research effort of Searle, they kept this faith. Maybe this will be a near miss too; maybe it won't help cancer, maybe most women will rely on the mysterious un-certainties of other ways to control birth, but there could be in Enovid an explosive combination and Searle's stockholders will continue to have faith.

It would be nice to say that phony growth always ends in disaster. But then how long does a person live? I have a friend who spent years in Buchenwald—he would have died there if his family had not had some extremely high con-nections in Sweden. Once we were talking about one of those Summit Conferences which obviously were not going to lead to any final settlement of East-West problems. He said, "Five years more alive—five years less dead." He was a European statistician with 14 generations of professors behind him. I was a naïve American—everything has to be done like Grant took Richmond. I have seen a lot of people make money out of phony growth stocks. I have seen them make money out of stocks whose growth qualities were partly real but which had been promoted so they were half or more phony. And I have seen a phony stock become real. I once looked at a company for a promoter—he let me buy some warrants for my trouble. I told him I thought it was overcapitalized. Time went by—it never made any money but it was bought in by a major company. I can't tell you the names without risking libel. The big company paid $24,000,000 for it in stock. I asked their major competitor if he could understand why. He said, "I thought they'd put the decimal in the wrong place." What the big company bought when it got the small company could not have been worth $24,000,000. They had no special technique; neither were they the technical leader in their field. There was absolutely no visible excuse to pay that vast sum for the little know-how the small company had but the stock of the big company had been kited to the skies by skillful promotion (all innocent, of course) and the naïve enthusiasm of "sophisticated" investors—especially managers of pension funds, mutual funds, etc.—so the underwriter, whose face resembles that of a good-humored bad wolf waiting for little Red Riding Hood, made a strictly legitimate fortune out of an investment in what was a not too technically able but thoroughly overcapitalized small company.

I can only tell you what I look for for myself: (1) I like to find some real reason why a product or service should grow fast enough to satisfy the high price I am probably going to have to pay for a growth stock. For instance, I bought High Voltage Engineering at 25. This looks cheap compared to the 200 it was bid at in early 1961 but at the time I bought it it was high compared to what I could get in more ordinary stocks—high, that is, in relation to tangible factors such as plant, sales, earnings, etc. So I spent a fair amount of time discussing their products with the management and getting a feeling why there might be an unusual future for them. High Voltage makes particle accelerators. These are machines which in various ways put a particle into motion (usually it is an electron or a proton but it might be an ion heavier than a proton) and delivers this accelerated particle to a target. The velocities of the particles develop energies which are measured in millions of volts. High Voltage had been founded by scientists from the Massachusetts Institute of Technology, one of whom was famous because he had invented the Van de Graaf electrostatic generator which was the heart of the Van de Graaf accelerator which, in turn, had played an important role in early atomic energy work; so I started my investigations with a feeling of respect for the scientific capability of the company.

Since I am a professional and since my Letter is a vehicle of publicity for companies, it is easy for me to get to see officers of corporations and spend virtually whatever time I want with them. I have been taken around in their private airplanes, put up at their guest houses, spend many long and delightful hours drinking with them, and in some cases our friendships changed from business friendships to very real personal attachments. But at any rate my professional status gives me an opportunity for getting to know a company which an ordinary investor cannot hope to have.

Fortunately for the ordinary investor this is not always the overwhelming advantage that it seems. As I have described before, the very informal relationships one develops as a professional can result in a type of myopic blindness. Moreover the time spent in getting to know something thoroughly means that you don't have time to think of other things which, though you may know them only superficially, you can make a lot of money on. My daughter Judy, for instance, said I should buy Mead Johnson—she had taken Metrecal and was crazy about it and she had the very sound idea that Mead Johnson would be a good buy. But I was too wrapped up in my own things to pay much attention. I made a dull mental note in my mind to look it up, but when I finally did it had gotten too high—or at least I thought it was too high. I could have easily solved the problem and bought the stock by reasoning this way: (1) Mead Johnson is a good company. (That's something which could be checked on from the records in a few minutes.) (2) It has a sensational new product—even if you are paying too much you aren't going to lose your shirt—so take a chance. But I didn't.

No matter how much time you spend on a situation you are always taking a chance, so if you aren't in a position to spend a great deal of time, you can clarify the situation simply by being willing to play a loose game and take a bigger chance (but one you are willing to take), and if you have a profit, either take it long before you should or take another sort of chance—stay with it for a long while and see if it doesn't work out big. Most people are always bothered by the fact that they either sell too soon and the stock goes much higher or they sell too late—and they look upward to where the stock once was. The basic principle of success in the market is to make a good profit when you make it but this doesn't mean you must sell within 95 per cent of the high or buy within 95 per cent of the low. Many professionals sell on the way down on purpose. They figure that no one will ever get the final high (well, maybe now and then, by luck) so you either sell before a stock makes its high or afterward. They like to see how high it will go before choosing how much less than the high they are going to get. So if you are not a professional don't try to play a tight game. Realize that your position requires a certain looseness in your approach, hopes, and demands. Try for good profits; it's very dangerous to be satisfied with small profits because inevitably at some time you will be facing a big loss, and so you must make good profits when you make them in order to stay ahead in your average operation. But don't try for fantastic profits; they may come to you by accident and welcome them when they do, but be happy with a basic operation which suits your real situation.

So if you don't have professional status, you can nevertheless get some clue, as my daughter gave me, as to why a new product might become big enough to justify the price. You can then quite easily, by applying standards of value analysis, ascertain how risky the company is and then you can decide if you wish to take a chance. Value analysis will not tell you when a stock is a good buy on the basis of growth but it will tell you something about the tangible factors; you can see from the record how long it has been in business, whether dividends have been paid and how steadily, what the earnings pattern is, how large the current assets are and how these compare to the current liabilities, what the capitalization is like, how much capital the company seems to need in relation to its sales, what the profit margin is like— these tangible facts can tell you whether you are looking at a well-established company with a new growth product or whether you are considering a new or poorly established company with growth possibilities. If you have a well-established company then, among other things, you know it won't have any trouble raising capital to exploit its new product. If it is not so well-established, then you know the management will have to be ingenious not to finance expansion by selling too much additional stock. These things you can gather from published material and then think over what the risks are and whether they are the sort you want to take.

And then there is the product—how do you find the growth

product? Some products which have grown in recent years and built fortunes for some people are: Chlorox, Tampax, Band-aids, penicillin and other antibiotics, electricity, telephones, airlines, missiles, particle accelerators, compact cars, text books, encyclopedias, plastic wrapping materials, nylon and other synthetic fibers, small private airplanes, solid state devices, cryogenic materials. Some of these are rather esoteric, some are extremely common—Kent Cigarette was just another cigarette but it made Lorillard a spectacular stock; among the greatest growth stocks of the past few years are book publishers—how old are books? Get out of your head the idea that growth has to occur in something rare or new; probably most growth does occur in something very new and most growth is in new companies but there are enough examples of growth in some established product because of some new force, or in some established company because of some new product, to make it worthwhile never to be academic about this essential force. Growth is worthwhile wherever you find worthwhile indications of it.

Sometimes you can have too much growth—as in the case of the oil companies. In 1952 oil stocks boomed because investors saw a well-defined 5-per-cent annual growth trend in consumption of petroleum and there was a scarcity of petroleum—or so they thought. Then huge new reserves were uncovered in Venezuela, Russia, and Libya and numerous minor discoveries were made elsewhere. Consumption has continued to grow, but there is no scarcity, and while the oil industry has controlled things fairly well, investors have become uncertain. Oil stocks did poorly from 1958 through 1961—at least that much of 1961 when this book was being written. What makes growth important to investors is not just growth but also a strange and not always too rational feeling of assurance that there will be almost endlessly growing profits—not a steady growth as I have said (investors are not always childish in what they want) but an assurance of eventual growth. And, as I have said before, this assurance does not spring up spontaneously—part of it comes out of informed quarters where not only is there a gift for statistics and economics but also for sponsorship and promotion. Stocks are not put up these days but belief is fostered.

So something made me believe in High Voltage. This something was the people I met, the sort of things I saw being made. I got a feeling of awe from the machines which were wonderfully new and of reality from the people as people. But they foxed me once: there was another company making particle accelerators on the West Coast; High Voltage didn't speak too highly of them, said they would go broke, which they all but officially did. When they were in financial difficulties High Voltage bought them in for $4,500,-000. I realized that the managers of High Voltage were capable of shrewd tactics as well as high science, so when they turned up their noses at Radiation Dynamics, I remembered what they had said about Arco and how Arco was actually a very fine company which if it had been just a bit more shrewdly or luckily led financially might have given High Voltage a hard time. So I looked into the situation carefully and listened carefully and bought Radiation Dynamics as well. I must admit that the votes have not been completely counted yet. My decision now is that even though High Voltage's management is not quite as pure in its every little thought as an electron, its shrewdness was undoubtedly one of the reasons for its success. The only danger facing it is that it may become too shrewd, or maybe it's more accurate to say—since the worth of shrewdness is also relative —that it may meet comparable combinations of scientific ability and shrewdness among its competitors.

In brief, to invest in growth you must somehow or other discover one of thousands of forms of reality that growth takes. You may be able to do this very simply by noticing some new thing that you and everyone else likes and finding out whether the company that provides it has stock trading on some stock market. You can check with your broker or bank as to whether it is a reasonably sound company or highly speculative or you can do some investigating yourself. Or you may find it in a very complex way, with very special advice or unusual personal knowledge. Or it may be thrust upon you the way some things have been thrust upon me. While I don't believe in formulas—perhaps because I am too literal and looking for too much in them—you may find formulas useful. They may have a meaning for you which however illogical it might seem to me leads you to the discovery of a valuable reality. The only way to judge any of your decisions is: are they profitable? Don't be ashamed of them if you were just lucky and don't be discouraged if you have a good many years of rather poor success. One of the mistakes the amateur makes is to overestimate the ability of the professional. I looked at the list of a mutual fund I know very well and saw that they had losses on 21 out of 40 selections—they were about even on six. I pointed out that this was not a great record. They agreed but they didn't feel too badly because where they had profits they had big ones. If you persist you will be successful.

CHAPTER TEN

What Is a Corporation?

Lawyers say a corporation is a legal person. They mean that for many purposes the courts will consider a corporation as a "person" or at least an entity separate from those who own or control it. Thus it has an independent life of its own, with rights, duties, and interests of its own, in the eyes of the law. Unlike a partnership, it can exist in perpetuity—it lives longer than ordinary persons. Like an individual, it can buy, sell, and hold property, sue and be sued, and so on. It can even sue its own managers if they misbehave. The American courts underwent a period of confused soul-searching before they fully worked out the status of a corporation as the concept of a legal person. But now it is a very well-established notion. In some rare instances—mostly when the corporation is owned by just one or a few persons—courts will abandon this carefully constructed fiction and hold the man behind the corporation responsible as if there were no corporation at all. They call this "piercing the corporate veil." By and large the veil is pretty substantial and real. Corporations are independent though non-corporeal individuals.

They are not, however, mechanical robots. They are owned by people, controlled by people, operated by people—at each stage of the game some living person does something or makes some decision which makes the non-corporeal individual work. *A corporation is actually a set of rules under which real people more efficiently get together and carry on some of their more important business and economic affairs.* It's a simple concept, but the subtleties of the matter may turn out to be a very complicated set of rules.

What are these rules? There is a 20-volume encyclopedia that lawyers use when they want to find out what rule applies to a particular situation—and this huge encyclopedia is just an index to thousands of reported decisions and numerous complicated statutes which vary widely from state to state.

A corporation is born by filing a charter, also called articles of incorporation, with the proper state authority. If you get a hungry lawyer, the whole thing can probably be managed in New York for $100. Once you have a charter—and there's no problem about getting one—you are on your way, legally, to becoming another General Motors or I.B.M.

This charter contains the rules of the corporation; for example, the number and kinds of stock, how many people on the Board of Directors, voting rights, and dozens of other basic matters. Most of the provisions are pretty well standardized—lawyers draft them by crossing out and substituting a few words and phrases in a copy of an old charter. To get through the legal gobbledygook is like walking knee-deep in spring mud.

One of the muddiest things in these charters is what's called the "powers" clauses, where an incredibly wordy effort is made to ensure that the corporation is empowered to do anything and everything it may ever want to do or actually do, even if by mistake. A typical line would be: "To sell, improve, manage, develop, lease, mortgage, dispose of, or otherwise turn to account, or deal with all or any part of the property of the corporation." When the lawyers are all done with pages and pages of this, they top the whole bit by adding a tag-line: "The foregoing enumeration of specific powers shall not be deemed to limit or restrict in any manner the general powers of the corporation"!

All this verbiage had a real purpose at one time. In the early days of corporations, lots of people who got stuck with bad deals, or just didn't want to pay up, would claim that the corporation was not empowered in its charter to enter into that particular kind of contract or transact that particular kind of business. Too often this argument—based on a high-class doctrine called *"ultra vires"*—worked, and the virtuous cheater didn't have to pay or live up to his deal. So the lawyers fixed that by adding more words—words to account for every possible and impossible eventuality.

So you send a dozen closely typed pages of ritualistic language to the Secretary of State in Albany or his counterpart in Dover, Delaware, along with the fee, and you have a corporate charter.

It didn't used to be so easy. The men who started the Hudson's Bay Company or the East India Company or any of the other great trading companies of the seventeenth century, which were the first of the modern corporations, had to put in a lot of effort and also money wheedling a Royal Charter out of one of the Stuart kings. And even in the nineteenth century, here in the United States, early corporate charters could be obtained only by a special act of a state legislature. Toward the end of the last century, the modern mass-production method of creating corporations began.

The states adopted corporation statutes which spelled out the how and the what, the do's and the don'ts, of the privilege of doing business forever without personal liability. For a time the states outbid each other by passing more and more favorable provisions of law. Finally Delaware went further than any of the others and ended up with most of the business. That is why most of the companies the public buys stocks in are Delaware corporations. The competition has died down. Now there are only occasional bursts of it—for instance, most mutual funds are incorporated in Maryland because that state passed a nicer law as far as the mutual-fund managers are concerned.

Among the vital provisions of the charter are those pertaining to its capitalization—it authorizes the directors of the corporation to borrow money, usually without definite limits, and to sell one or more types of stock, preferred or common usually, within defined limits. For instance, it might authorize a company to borrow $1,000,000 (if it can) and sell 1,000,000 shares of common stock. With this authority the corporation might then borrow $500,000 and sell 500,000 shares of common to finance its initial projects. If it required additional financing, its directors have the authority to authorize borrowing additional money or selling additional stock up to the limits of the charter's authorization.

After charters, there are bylaws. They contain more detailed rules than the charter, but most of them are still general enough to be pretty well standardized. For instance, the bylaws say who the officers shall be and enumerate certain broad powers and limitations of office. They also ordinarily provide for the occasions and the conduct of directors' and shareholders' meetings, registration and transfer of stock, etc. There is a certain overlap of regulatory provisions which may be put in the charter or, with some companies, in the bylaws. A rule has somewhat more status if it is in the charter.

But both the charter and the bylaws require a shareholder's vote to be amended (except for rare instances). For instance, if the managers want to increase the number of authorized shares, they have to get your approval as a stockholder—but not if they want to issue already authorized shares to raise more money or, say, in exchange for the shares of some other company as a means of effecting a merger. They have to ask your permission to increase the number of directors on the Board or to create a new post such as honorary chairman of the Board where an aging leader can retire in comfort. Some of the things they have to ask stockholder authorization for are trivial, while some of those they have the inherent authority to conclude, such as the purchase of the assets or part of the assets of another corporation, are of vital importance. The importance of the stockholder's vote varies—sometimes you have the choice of black or white; sometimes you have that of varying shades of gray.

Lawyers say that the thing to remember about the development of any body of law, including the much-litigated and much-legislated field of corporate law, is that the courts and the legislators move slowly, they're always behind the times, but eventually they do try to come to terms with realities. Not usually in a direct way, though. They putter and mend and modify rather than redoing the whole thing. They seldom abandon a rule or principle but just let it hang on—with the result that there are a lot of ancient and probably unnecessary rules around. For example, it is a firm principle that the Directors are responsible for what the corporation does, for managing its business—not the stockholders and not the officers, but the Board of Directors acting as a body. Now as a matter of fact, the corporation is actually run by a group of officers, some of whom will also be members of the Board, which constitutes the "management." So the practice got established where officers would carry through on a deal and then, after it was done, present it to the Board for approval. In adjusting to the fact of life that a cumbersome Board cannot really carry on the business of a corporation, the courts have accepted the validity of this ritualistic *ex post facto* ratification of transactions.

They also have allowed the Board to delegate a great deal of responsibility to a smaller, more maneuverable executive committee, which runs things at the crucial level where policy and administration meet. Then every month or so the full Board, which includes leading citizens with extensive interests elsewhere, meets maybe for lunch, maybe they serve coffee, and ratifies everything the executive committee and the officers have done. But by hanging on to the fiction that the full Board runs things, the law makes them responsible if anything goes wrong. When an irate stockholder sues for mismanagement, he sues the whole Board. In order to get distinguished men to serve under these circumstances, managements have gotten the stockholders to approve charter or bylaw provisions designed to indemnify directors and officers who are held liable for damages to the corporation. The S.E.C. doesn't care for these provisions at all—especially when they cover mishandling of a registration—but the state legislatures and the courts have gone along with them to a considerable extent. That's the way the law works. Law rhymes with seesaw.

But let's get back to what the shareholder's vote means. Besides getting the right to vote on changes of the charter or bylaws, the management also has to come to you if it wants to merge with another company, or dissolve the corporation and go out of business, or reduce the capital, or sell all or a substantial part of the assets, or a number of other big moves like that. On merger or sale you are apt to get, besides a vote, the right of appraisal—that is, if you don't like the terms of the deal, you can ask a court to decide the cash value of your stock and receive that instead. You also get the right to vote sometimes when the law and the charter don't require that you get it: the management may want a majority of the stockholders to ratify their action, just as the Board of Directors typically does. This looks good if they ever have to go to court to defend their doings; it's frequently done when they grant profitable stock options or employment contracts or other big benefits to themselves.

Sounds impressive, this stockholders' vote, but don't be fooled. Despite all the Fourth of July talk about "stockholders' democracy" and all the hysterical efforts of the famous Gilbert Brothers (and others), it doesn't come to very much. Because your ownership of that piece of paper does not in reality amount to ownership of the corporation itself or ownership of what the corporation owns. (All you own is your limited position in the broad and complicated set of rules which we have decided is what a corporation is.) What is missing is control—and that is the core of ownership.

Probably the greatest part of the more than 1,000 corporations whose securities are listed on the New York Stock Exchange are under what is called "management control." Which means that a key group of top executives dominates the Board of Directors, which is supposed to run the company, and can deliver the majority vote of the stockholders, who are supposed to elect the Directors and own the company. A handful of these listed companies (the total of which employed 20 per cent of civilian workers in 1957, owned 30 per cent of assets invested in private business, and accounted for 35 per cent of corporate sales) are still two-thirds or better owned by one man or a single, close group. A large number are operated under what is called "working control" —where something between 20–30 per cent and 50 per cent of the stock is owned by a cohesive group which is also management or part of management.

The management runs things, whether or not it owns the

things it runs. More and more the ownership of things tends to become irrelevant when you think about this first and foremost quality of property, the right to control it—use it or misuse it. If money isn't money any more, neither is property —especially securities. Some of the biggest management-controlled outfits are beginning to admit the fact that their managements are not mere humble hired hands of the stockholders. The giant of giants, A.T.&T.—with 1,600,000 stockholders, the biggest of which holds not more than 1/30 of 1 per cent—has advanced the idea that the function of its management is sort of to mediate between the interests of the employees, stockholders, suppliers, customers, and the community in general. They have stopped making believe that a share in $21,000,000,000 of assets is like a partnership in a corner grocery store.

But these independent managements still live up to the law by holding stockholder meetings to re-elect themselves each year. If you own one share, you are entitled to attend and vote in person.

Most of the vote has already come in by mail. Prior to a stockholders' meeting the company mails the stockholders a ballot—called a proxy—and with the proxy goes a notice of the call to meeting and an agenda for the meeting. In the old days brokerage houses voted the proxies of the shares which they held even though the shares were held for the accounts of various customers and they voted the way they wanted, which was usually in favor of the management, unless otherwise instructed by a customer. This has changed. If you keep your stock with your broker, he will mail you the proxy and notice of meeting which a company has sent for him to mail and he will also request that you vote the proxy yourself; otherwise it won't be voted at all. While you can vote against the management if you wish, very few stockholders do—for one thing there very seldom is an opposition party or program to vote for. Relatively few shares are represented by the stockholders who actually attend a meeting in person, and while there are always some complaints, managements have learned to listen to them politely because even when the complaints are justified or the suggestions for change worth considering, a management can feel certain at least 95 per cent of the time that the proxies mailed in are predominantly in their favor.

Lately some of the bigger corporations—on advice of stockholder relations counsel—have turned these drab meetings into elaborately well-staged (and much more enjoyable) entertainments. There are tasty box lunches, sometimes movies, as well as dull speeches. Recently one of the railroads offered bargain rates for travel to and accommodations at a resort hotel it owned: the response was such that the offer had to be repeated. Another company held its meeting simultaneously in a dozen or more cities by means of closed-circuit TV. Like annual reports to stockholders—which have been pictorially dressed up in recent years—the annual meeting is now understood to be a great opportunity to build up the "corporate image," get across the company's story, and maybe incidentally boost the price of the stock.

Ninety-nine out of 100 times the management nominates and solicits proxies for the election or re-election of an unopposed slate of Directors. In other words, most often corporate democracy so-called operates under a one-party system where your only choice is not whom to vote for but whether to vote at all. (Incidentally, if a majority of the stockholders "stay away" by not sending in their proxies and there is no quorum, the old Board holds over until a quorum can be gotten together—so usually the non-vote doesn't come to anything either.)

The few idealists who object to this dim view of "stockholders' democracy" all insist that any stockholder can form a "second party" and put forward his own nominees and thus exercise the purported control-feature inhering in his stock certificate. Sure he can—but he seldom can elect them.

The two-party system in corporate affairs really comes to life only when there is a "raid" on the company or an actual proxy contest, and most often the two go together. A raid is an attempt by an outside syndicate to buy enough stock in the company so that the insiders, the management, are forced to deal with them and share or surrender control of the company. A buying campaign of this kind is followed by an actual proxy contest—where both the insiders and the outsiders solicit the other stockholders for proxies to elect opposing slates of Directors—when the management decides to fight instead of compromise or surrender. When there is a struggle for control of a corporation, both sides buy as much stock as they can, get friendly parties to buy stock, and make all-out efforts to line up other big holders. They particularly go after brokers and investment bankers who swing a lot of weight through their influence on wealthy customers.

The buying campaigns are of course extremely expensive—and risky, because all that buying boosts the price of the stock artificially. A proxy campaign is also expensive—some big ones have cost one side alone almost $1,000,000, not counting the millions that must be ponied up for the buying campaign. It is decidedly not an activity to be contemplated by the ordinary investor.

A struggle for control, in other words, is between an inside giant and an outside giant—and neither giant bothers with the ordinary pygmy stockholder unless the negotiations between them fall through. There are probably a hundred buying campaigns for every proxy contest. And when there is a real contest, with expensive soliciting campaigns and newspaper advertising and all the other paraphernalia, what are you—the 100-share stockholder—being asked to decide? On the deficit side, the incumbent management is perhaps stodgy—they've been living unimaginatively off that particular hog a little too long. The outsiders are apt to be more modern and aggressive; maybe they even have some good new managerial and financial notions, but note that they will have to recoup their expenses one way or the other, they will have made promises and incurred obligations to friends which will have to be honored, and maybe they are in the business of raiding and will use the company's assets to buy stock in some other corporation in furtherance of a subsequent raid. You can be certain they didn't spend a lot and risk a lot in order to do *you* a favor. Raiders tend to go after companies which have slowed down and are in an excessive liquid position—the first because otherwise they can't be caught and the second because otherwise there isn't enough worth catching.

You can take it as gospel that an "in" group can be dislodged only when there is disastrous mismanagement or very unfavorable business conditions. A large group of stockholders will always vote for the management, on rainy days and sunny days, just out of habit. And the ins are allowed to use corporate money and patronage in their fight to stay in—which is a real difference from a regular political campaign. Only a big syndicate, with purposes of its own, is capable even in extreme circumstances of flushing out any management, even a poor one. One law professor put it this way: "The modern proxy contest is at best a device for tempering autocracy by invasion." And that about sums it up.

The most practical thing to do if you have a stock which is going up because of a proxy contest is to sell out and count your blessings. The ordinary stockholder, who might be someone who owned 100 shares of Cessna Aircraft or 10,000 shares of American Telephone—in either case his percentage of ownership and therefore his vote would be small in relation to the total—doesn't know enough about the problems of the business he has invested in to have an effective vote either on the basis of his interest in the company or his understanding of its problems or his personal knowledge of the abilities of the management or of those who may want to become the new management.

The "control" you get through your stockholder's vote can therefore be ignored. Because it isn't really there. True control resides with management because it is management, or with a large bloc of stock because it is large enough to select management. The control factor, even when it comes directly from stock ownership, is a feature of the bloc, of the aggregate of shares owned, not of each individual share with its single vote. It is obvious that a bloc of 51 per cent of all the stock would have control, but in practice blocs much smaller than that have control. This is because an individual officer realizes that a bloc of 20 per cent or 30 per cent of the stock has a big-enough interest in the company and knows enough about it and probably commands other resources of a magnitude capable of unseating an officer if he bucks it. Moreover, usually such a bloc is held by people who started the company or who somehow got control of it years ago and who have over the years carefully selected officers to do their bidding. Thus bloc control can be real control even though it is a minority of the total stock outstanding.

This fact is beginning to be recognized by the courts. So they have held, for instance, that if a control bloc is sold in excess of market, what was sold was not just the collection of individual shares but also the control feature of the bloc itself. And this is not supposed to be sold because it is not supposed to exist, control being the technical prerogative of the Board of Directors as such. There have been cases where the court has required the selling group to return to the corporation or the other stockholders the difference between the special price for the bloc and the actual market value of the individual shares comprising the bloc. And if the group that buys control milks the corporation by means of the control it bought, the court may hold the selling group liable for the damage to the corporation. This development in the law really pins it down and proves that control is control. So there it is—you get a vote when you buy a share of stock, and after reading this you know what to do with it.

Your stock certificate, or bond or any other piece of corporate paper you buy, is a contract. It represents a deal between you and the company. That's what you buy when you purchase corporate paper—an agreement. But not all the terms of the agreement are written out on the piece of paper you get. For instance, the usual bond contains a fine-print summary of the terms of the deal and refers to the indenture under which the bond was issued—and these run to the size of a book. The special and elaborate provisions of an issue of preferred stock will be contained in the charter and maybe also in resolutions of the Board of Directors. So the terms of your actual contract may be spread around in a number of places. But the certificate, whether of common or preferred stock or of a bond, will contain a statement informing you where to look for the full exposition of your agreement.

The kinds of deals a corporation can make with its paperholders are limited somewhat by corporation statutes and other state and federal laws, but mostly only by the ingenuity of the mind of man. Moreover, one corporation may have several different kinds of securities in the hands of the public (and several more in private hands).

The broadest distinction between types of securities is supposed to be equity as contrasted with debt paper. That is the difference between common stock and a bond. But some preferred shares are more like a bond than a share, and convertible debentures are more like shares than a bond. These hybrid instruments have proliferated and become more popular in recent years. It's helpful to remember that the terms of corporate paper can be mixed up like chop suey, and you have to look to the actual terms and not merely the official designation of the certificate.

It might also be helpful, perhaps, to set down some definitions here, along with some discussion of the various kinds of instruments you may be buying. Here's a little glossary:

A *bond* is a generic term for a debt, like the word "note." What you buy is a beautifully engraved piece of paper which says the corporation owes you, for instance, $1,000. The corporation suggests that it will repay the debt 10 or 20 years from the date of issue, and meanwhile will pay 5-per-cent interest quarterly or semi-annually. That's simple enough, but that's only the bare beginning. The bond is issued under an indenture, which is a book-length contract governing all conceivable aspects of the future relations among the bondholders, the corporation, and the trustee (usually a bank) which "represents" and is empowered to act for the whole group of bondholders in most dealings with the corporation. The provisions of the indenture are fairly well standardized—some are required by the S.E.C.—and most of them are minor and technical. The main thing to know about a debt is whether it is secured, if so by what, and its standing in relation to other debts of the corporation; that is, what is senior or junior to it. Also of interest is whether the indenture calls for a sinking fund to ensure that there will be money available when the time comes to pay off the debt. And then there are income bonds, which provide for no set rate of interest but only so much as may be earned (with a ceiling, of course). Bondholders vote only on rare occasions and then only with respect to the debt and its administration, never on general corporate matters. Bonds go up and down in price just as do stocks, but there is one significant difference. You can have a very large paper loss in the best grade of bond not because the bond itself is not good but because the national structure of interest rates has changed. The interest-rate structure is changed at least partially at will by the central banking authority which in our country is the Federal Reserve Board. After World War II the government began to restrict the money supply and this resulted in higher interest rates; after the Korean War this effort was increased so that interest rates about doubled between 1945 and 1960. This has brought about a very serious decline in the market price of long-term bonds sold to the public years ago. Of course when the day for redemption rolls around, the bond, if high grade, is sure to be paid off so the loss is temporary if the owner doesn't have to sell in the meanwhile.

A *convertible* security is a debt or stock instrument that can be exchanged for another kind of security. The most popular form in recent years has been the convertible debenture (*see* definition below) which is a debt that can be changed into common stock at a specified price and sometimes also at specified times in the future. This instrument has been very attractive as a hedge: while you're waiting to see how the company is going to do, you retain status as a creditor, and if the company prospers, you can switch over to being an owner. The price of convertible debentures tends to fluctuate closely in line with the price movements of the

common stock of the corporation. With a convertible security—especially a bond or preferred—you are better protected
on the down-side than if you owned stock, without losing all
the chances for big gain on the up-side that may go with an
equity security.

Other types of bonds and preferred stock may also contain
a conversion feature; and recently two classes of common,
one of which can be converted into the other, have become
well known. For instance, a Class B stock may be issued to
the controlling stockholders of a company which will not be
entitled to receive dividends for some years or which may not
ever receive dividends but which may at some future time be
converted to Class A which the public holds and which is
entitled to receive dividends immediately. The controlling
stockholders being, perhaps, officers of the company or otherwise having very large incomes may not want dividends because they realize that most of the dividend will be taxed
away by Uncle Sam, but the public stockholder who may not
have such a large income may want dividends. Thus adequate dividends can be paid to the ordinary stockholder
while the controlling group foregoes them and builds up the
economy. This type of two-class common can serve a constructive purpose or can be promotional.

Suppose a company has 1,000,000 shares outstanding di-
vided half into B and half into A. Suppose it is earning one
dollar a share but needs money for expansion. It can afford
to pay 50 cents a share on A because it is paying out only
25 per cent of all that it is earning on the combined shares. If
there were only one class of stock, it could not afford to pay
out 50 cents a share. Thus this generous pay-out to the public may have the effect of building up the company, but it
also may have the effect of giving a false picture of the basic
long-term dividend-paying potential of the company. Some

day the holders of B are going to convert their shares into A. Promotional groups use this type of stock set-up to kite the dividend-paying stock and then they slyly convert and sell out. But sincere groups also use this type of capitalization for constructive purposes. There is nothing mystical about a convertible instrument—it is really just two pieces of paper in one, the conversion feature being nothing more than an option (*see* definition below) which could be—and frequently is—a separate piece of paper.

A *debenture*, whether convertible or unconvertible, is a special kind of bond, one that is secured only by the general credit of the corporation—not by any specific assets. It is also usually a junior obligation, which means some other bonds (or debts) get paid off first if the company gets into trouble. If you really want to know how secure your security is, you will in the case of a debenture have to look at the "subordination" provisions of the indenture. Some debentures are subordinate to anything the corporation has already borrowed or decided to borrow in the future. These technical provisions and differences are not important unless a company gets into trouble—unless a nation suffers a severe and prolonged depression, very few important companies get into serious difficulties. This is even more true today than in former years because most important companies are run by professionally trained managements, and while such managements have their faults, they usually escape the gross errors of mismanagement which plague smaller companies and used to plague large, family-dominated companies. When a company does get into difficulties, there are usually so many complex aspects to the particular situation that too high respect for the "book learning" aspect of a legal technicality can be something of a handicap in the formation of an investment judgment. One good rule for the average investor is not to buy any bond or debenture unless you are told by a reliable authority that it is truly high grade. Since bonds are rated AAA, AA, A, ABB, etc., by competent rating agencies, it isn't hard to find out whether a bond is in the high-grade range or beneath it.

Preferred stock represents an ownership share in a corporation, technically, but it is really more like a debenture than common stock. Ordinarily preferred stock receives its dividend before the common, and at a stated rate, say 6 per cent. Frequently dividends on the preferred are cumulative —that is, if not paid because not earned in one year, the arrearage has to be paid in subsequent years before the common is entitled to get anything. So this kind of stock is "preferred" as to dividends. It can be, and most often is, "preferred" also in any liquidation of assets—preferred over the common, that is, not over debts. It is often subject to call and early retirement at a premium, although it does not ordinarily carry a definite retirement date. Most preferred stock does not have voting rights, except under certain specified conditions, like a continuing failure to pay required dividends. It can, of course, be convertible, although this is not usual. Preferred stock is considered a "safer" investment than common and fluctuates in value somewhat as bonds do, only more so.

An *option* is a contract that gives you the right to buy or sell something in the future but does not carry the obligation to do so. When you pay for an option, you are in effect buying the privilege of making up your mind later as to whether you want to enter into a particular deal at a price and on the terms already decided upon.

Puts and *calls* are, respectively, sell and buy options. When you buy a put you get the right to sell certain stock at a set price within a particular time period. They are ordinarily bought by investors who own and intend to hold some of the same stock, but are worried enough about a possible down-movement to pay for the privilege of protecting themselves. A call is the opposite of a put—the right to buy—and might be purchased by someone who sold some stock and wanted to hedge against the possibility of a rise in its market value. People speculate in puts and calls without reference to their other holdings.

If it is an option, say, to buy 100 shares of some stock within six months at $10 a share, you will have to pay for the option now. Later on, if you make up your mind to exercise the option, you will have to pay $1,000 for the stock. Thus if you paid $200 for the option, the stock will cost you $1,200 altogether, or $12 a share. However, if for some reason the stock is selling at $15 a share, you can immediately sell it and make a $300 profit. This would be a high rate of profit on the $200 you invested in the option. I have known people who made a great deal of money on the type of option which is commonly dealt in in Wall Street. I have had only fair luck myself, and most people don't have much luck at all. It takes a very keen sense of timing to make money on the short-term options which are called puts, calls, straddles, etc. If you are interested in long-term development, you probably won't be so interested in puts and calls. Option is a generic term. Other types are strips, straps, and straddles. Rights and warrants are a different type of option. (*See* definitions below.)

Put and call options can be purchased in a proliferation of forms. For example, a "straddle" which is both—an option to buy *or* sell the same stock at the same price. Or a "spread" which is like a straddle except the buy and sell prices differ. And some newer cute ones: a "strip" is a straddle with an extra put, and a "strap" is a straddle with an extra call. A word of warning about *selling* options: if your call is called, you have to have the stock to deliver; and if a put you sold is exercised, you have to have the money to put up for the stock being tendered. Of course, if you buy options—well, it just costs money, like everything else.

Rights are also options of a kind. They are issued by the corporation itself, most often without charge to its own stockholders. This is the way the company gives its existing stockholders the opportunity to buy a pro rata share of a new issue of securities. This may be required by the charter (and in some states by law) if that basic document provides for what are called "pre-emptive rights"—designed to give stockholders some protection against dilution of their holdings. If the recipient of the right does not want to buy more stock or does not have the ready cash, he can sell it—so a pre-emptive right provision in the charter is worth something. (That is, if it's a successful corporation.) *Warrants* are like rights, but they are most often sold as speculative paper by the corporation to other than its existing stockholders; they may also be attached to other securities. Rights ordinarily must be exercised within a short period, but warrants may remain viable for a much longer time. Warrants usually originate when a security has to be sold under dubious market conditions or when, under even good market conditions, the security has a dubious future—after a stock market crash, for instance, when it is hard to get investors to buy anything—or they are attached to an offering of a speculative stock by the underwriters. Some stocks with dubious futures represent soundly and sincerely run companies engaged in a highly hazardous enterprise like the development of a new mine or wildcatting for oil. Some represent highly dubious people. Very often the underwriter (or investment banker) who sponsors a highly speculative company is given warrants as part of his compensation. When you investigate a stock, see if there are any warrants, rights, or options outstanding. If there are and if these give their owners the right to buy a substantial amount of the stock at some future date, then you should figure how much stock there will be outstanding when these options are exercised in order to get a true idea of how much the company may eventually be able to earn per share or is now earning per share. But like all such advice, this often doesn't do the investor much good. If a company does extremely well, it may not make much difference how many options there are and how much dilution this means; whereas a company which does only fairly well may not represent a good investment even though it is conservatively capitalized. But warrants, calls, options, etc., are things to look for, and if there is a public market in them, they are sometimes a better buy than the stock itself. This is because you pay less for them. If things turn out very well for the stock, you can subscribe to the stock at the price named on the warrant—or you can just sell your warrant and you'll find that you have made a higher percentage on your capital. If things turn out not so well, you may lose a higher percentage too.

Stock, if no other adjective is involved, will usually mean *common* stock. But it also is sometimes called capital stock. This is an accounting nicety and is meaningless so far as practical investing is concerned. Common stock is an expressive term though—it isn't preferred, it isn't special in any way, it is common. Sometimes common stock has been issued as a bonus to the people who put the original money in a company—it costs them nothing. Very often the original stock issued to the original investors costs them very little. They may get it for some sort of effort—legal, scientific, underwriting—or because they contributed land or patents or because they bought bonds or preferred stock and thus gave the company the money to get started.

If a company succeeds, the earnings above those amounts claimed by bondholders or other preferred investors belong to the common stockholders. They may be paid out as dividends or collected as part of the earned surplus of the company. The company may—probably will—use these retained earnings to finance the continued growth of the company. This surplus plus the amount originally paid for the common —if any was paid—plus that paid in later years when additional common was sold to various investors, plus various not-too-important accounting adjustments, make up what is called the equity of the corporation. Common shares are often called equities because they have a claim to all values not specifically reserved for the various grades of investments with defined value. You are buying a share in a living organism—the equity of a business—whose value is subject to rather rapid change; in most years this change is reasonably good—in some years the company loses and the equity shrinks.

With money and common stock you have the two basic contracts in our "free contract" capitalistic society. With this important difference: that when you go to dispose of common stock paper, it may be worth a good deal more or a good deal less than when you acquired it; but when you dispose of money paper, it has had since 1940 a much better chance to be worth a little bit less than when you got it. Many sophisticated people are not clearly aware that common stock is a form of money. More stock can be issued in exchange for assets of another business; options can be granted to key employees or others who may be important to the company— these options in some cases can be sold, in others give the owner a chance some day to cash in on a big capital gain.

Stocks are not the official money of a capitalist country but they are an essential part of the total capitalist money system. In 1960 the stocks listed for trading on the New York Stock Exchange alone had a market value of almost $300,000,000,-000. Their value about equaled that of the National Debt. Of course their value was subject to rapid change; the National Debt is much more solid. Still the balance was interesting.

The great historical principle of freedom of contract includes, among other things, the sweeping privilege of making a fool out of yourself. It became such a popular pastime during the Twenties, especially with respect to securities, that finally the federal government had to step in and limit the excessive freedom of the securities market. This followed the famous Pecora investigation of the securities business, which resulted in the New Deal regulatory legislation administered by the Securities and Exchange Commission. At the beginning, the S.E.C. and its statutory arsenal (which has since been augmented) were viewed by the financial community like a foreign army that had invaded these hallowed shores. But in the 27 years that have passed since the Securities Act of 1933 was put into effect, people in the securities business and corporate managers have learned to live with this system of regulation. In fact they rather like it: after the first flush of righteous indignation, everybody who isn't stealing feels a little more comfortable when there is a cop on the block.

S.E.C. regulation tends to create an official, sanitary image of the securities business in the public's mind—despite the fact that the Commission goes to great lengths to assure the public that it does not approve or disapprove any securities. Every prospectus must contain a legend to this effect in bold-face type on the cover sheet. Somewhat contradicting the assertion of this legend is the fact that the Commission can and on occasion does refuse to allow an issue to be sold to the public. The basis for any such refusal—called a "stop order"—is never that the Commissioners feel the particular stock is not a good buy or even that it is worthless paper. Federal law does not prohibit the sale of worthless paper—it merely requires that the fact of worthlessness and the reasons for it be clearly stated in the prospectus and that everyone who is offered the paper be given a copy of this document.

The primary thrust of the federal securities law is full public disclosure of all relevant information. There is a good deal more to it, but that's the heart of the matter. So to get the full benefit of the law you have to read, and know how to read, the information that is disclosed to you as a member of the investing public.

If a corporation supplies false or misleading information in response to S.E.C. requirements, or if it fails to disclose everything called for, the security holder can sue for his damages. But this privilege is limited by a short statute of limitations, so no time should be wasted. It is, however, easier to win a suit under the federal law than it is to make out a full case of fraud under ordinary law. (If you think you've been had, the best thing is to overcome your embarrassment and run to a lawyer right away. Next best: identify yourself as an indignant and injured member of the great American investing public and complain to the Stock Exchange itself— especially if your indignity involves a member thereof.)

Some of the filings required by the Commission must be made available directly to each security holder; others are just "filed"—they become public documents, available at certain offices of the S.E.C. but not distributed widely. The main ones that are widely distributed are the prospectus, the proxy statement, and the annual report.

The prospectus is required whenever securities are offered for sale to the public in more than one state. It is part of a registration statement which is just "filed" in Washington and which contains some frequently interesting material as, for instance, full copies of all substantial agreements regarding the affairs of the corporation, some of which are summarized in the more widely distributed prospectus. This document, usually a 20- to 40-page booklet, contains a history of the company, if any; what the company makes, what it owns, and something about its position in the industry; up-to-date financial statements and a history of earnings, if any; summaries of long-term contracts and of material transactions of recent vintage; and the scoop about the promoters, owners, and top officers. Each time a new issue of securities is offered, a new registration statement—or the old one brought up to date—must be filed. If there are regular offerings, as with most utility companies (and other big companies because of stock option plans for the top managers), the sequence of registration statements with exhibits provides a continuing fundamental history of the company.

The annual report in recent years has become a beautifully gotten up sales message, usually with pictures. The management writes the report—it usually is signed by the president and/or the chairman of the Board of Directors—and naturally the report puts every management decision in its best light. For instance, an annual report never says anything like this:

A bitter six months strike resulted in our losing all the profits we had earned in the first half. The strike lasted as long as it did because I and other members of the management want to subordinate the union. We did not feel the demands of the union were actually unfair—it's hard to see why those who work for the company as labor should not wish to earn 15 cents more an hour, especially when we of the management have free transportation in the company's cars and airplanes, live free in the company's hotel suites and guest houses, and in addition to our pension funds and salaries have in the last half dozen years persuaded you—dear stockholders—to vote us stock options by which we can buy, whenever profitable, 5 per cent of the stock of the company. No, the desires of the workers seemed pitifully modest—it made us feel again that one of the things wrong with humanity is its lack of widespread, large-scale ambition. What we fought the strike for was to lick Richard Casey, the head of the Union, and Dave Cohen, the union lawyer. These men, like us, are ambitious, vigorous, hard-driving business sophisticates—we decided they must be defeated and so we sacrificed our profits for the year to do this. The union members, their wives, and children spent a miserable six months; they will take years to gain in wage increases what they lost in the strike, but this has made them work all the harder now that they are back.

This is never written in an annual report nor is anything ever put down which gives us a penetrating insight to the human drama which is a company. Even if a company president were a writer, the corporation lawyers would see that he didn't exercise his talents in an annual report. The report is a means by which management successes are emphasized and management failures are rationalized, lightly touched on, or ignored. It is, therefore, one of the ways by which management stays in power. But some managements are very able and some of the things done and mentioned in the report are of true significance.

The financial statements—the income account, balance sheet, depreciation and maintenance accounts, if given—can be of great significance to those trained and experienced enough to understand them. But these, too, can be tidied up. In general, as soon as a management is adequately aware of what investors want, they give them as good a semblance as they can. For instance, investors these days approve of high research expenditures; therefore some managements throw every expense that they can into the research account. If they have a company cafeteria and this is next to the research wing, then this is included in research expense.

The proxy statement, which calls for disclosure of the more unpleasant kinds of information like how much salary the officers received (an item not mentioned in the report), deals of the company involving top officers, directors, or big stockholders, and so on, is not so beautifully gotten up. In fact, they are as unreadably written as legal artistry can make them. (The S.E.C. requires "disclosure"—not writing that can be read painlessly.) The proxy statement also contains background information on any matter relating to which your vote is being solicited, if any action at the stockholders' meeting beyond election of Directors is intended. If no special action is on the agenda, they run to about three or four rather closely printed pages; if something like a sale or merger is under consideration, they may be as fat as a prospectus. Annual reports and proxy statements are required of all companies whose securities are listed on an exchange. Such listed companies must also file additional reports which are not sent out to security holders—as fuller financial information than that in the annual report is filed on form 10K; form 8K whenever certain important events take place; a semi-annual earnings statement on form 9K; and others.

The S.E.C. accomplishes a great deal more directly and indirectly in policing the securities market than has been mentioned. It administers the Public Utility Holding Company Act of 1935, which was considered the end of the world when it was enacted. This act has more direct regulation than mere disclosure in it. There is also the Trust Indenture Act of 1939, which requires most debt issues to be trusted, and prescribes certain terms of the trust. The Commission also regulates securities markets, investment companies, and investment advisors, in certain regards. It can initiate criminal prosecution for fraud and other illegal activities in interstate commerce.

Besides the S.E.C., the security markets are policed by the stock exchanges themselves, and in the case of stocks which are not listed on a stock exchange, policing is done by the National Association of Security Dealers. The effectiveness of this policing depends in part on the serious-mindedness of the investing public. But the investing public is just the same old public that goes to the circus. That fact is that, for a while at least, people sometimes make money by doing the wrong thing—by investing on tips, by buying crazy speculative stocks, etc. Since people don't live indefinitely but only for a while, this sector of their lives during which they make money magically and feel like trillionaires is a sector which they should perhaps not be deprived of. It is quite easy to avoid tragic loss of fortune in the stock market simply by owning what you buy, by diversifying your holdings and applying rules of security analysis which you can get from a book like this and many others. You can be safer in stocks than in any other form of investment—this is because you can diversify more readily. But safety is not what everyone wants. When your objective becomes something which involves danger, then you are in danger whether the market is policed or not. You cannot expect to make the sort of money which an insider makes when you are an outsider. Now and then people do, but the people in the market have some control as to what goes on—not of the market as a whole but in relation to particular companies and their stocks. They are never going to deal with the public with the affectionate feminine fairness of a nursery school teacher. The authorities try to make them do that, but the people they are trying to give a nursery-school psychology to are a pretty tough set of men. Don't let their Brooks Brothers suits fool you.

To highlight the whole matter, I might just mention Section 16 of the Securities Exchange Act of 1934. This requires directors, officers, and principal stockholders of listed companies—colloquially known as "insiders"—to file monthly statements of their transactions in the stock of the companies as to which they are "insiders." To keep them from using inside information to their profit (in the old days this was a way of life) they are absolutely liable to the corporation for any short-term (less than six months) profit they may make on either the purchase and sale, or sale and purchase, of an equity security of the company they are inside.

Big Brother is looking out for you. The question is do you want to hold his hand when you are making money as tightly as you do when you are losing it? This Big Brotherness means a substantial abridgement of the freedom to contract, but it is all to the advantage of the weaker of the contracting parties—namely, you. Like most government regulation in our "free enterprise" society, it does not make everything 100 per cent right, but being a practical response to particular abuses as they developed, it definitely makes those particular abuses less attractive to the abusers, and so the abusers have to think harder. Generally speaking it keeps the people who are running things from running away with things.

The S.E.C. based on federal power is the big gun in securities regulation. But, as I have said, there are some other types of scattered artillery worth mentioning. I will try to elaborate but briefly.

The New York Stock Exchange no longer needs much prodding from the S.E.C. to exercise the strictest kind of financial inspection and other bookkeeping supervision over its member firms. It is considered the best form of good business to ensure that these firms use the securities and money entrusted to them in proper ways, and that they so operate generally as to remain in good financial condition. The solvency record of member firms has been almost perfect since 1939 and has been better than the record for U.S. banks as a group since before that.

The Exchange enforces reporting and other rules for all listed companies—that is, supervision over the stock it sells as well as the brokers and dealers who handle the transactions. For example, in order to qualify for listing, a company must have earning power of $1,000,000 after taxes, net tangible assets of over $8,000,000, and 400,000 shares held by not less than 1,500 shareholders. (The criteria for de-listing are however much lower.) It has for many years refused to list non-voting common stock—which probably as much as anything else has kept this kind of security from becoming important in the U.S. as it has in some European countries. The rules of the Big Board are much stricter than on other exchanges, but all exchanges operate under controls—because of the federal law and in order to present a good face to the public.

Federal financial agencies not connected with the S.E.C. exercise both direct and indirect control over the money available for the purchase of securities. If the authorities feel that the security market is running away with itself, they can—and they have—raised margin requirements to 100 per cent. (The Exchange itself regulates maintenance-of-margin requirements.) It is generally assumed that thin margins contributed greatly to the precipitate collapse of the 1929 bull market, and responsible brokerage houses are glad that this particular potential-for-disaster has long been eliminated.

Not only the federal government but most of the states have laws governing the issuance and sale of securities. The state rules are charmingly described as "blue sky" laws—which denotes their general purpose, to keep the price of securities and notions of value and salesmanship methods more or less earthbound. The statutory schemes of the states are different from that of the federal government, being not so devoted to disclosure as the one technique of control. The state laws vary widely, from *pro forma* registration of a new issue sold within the jurisdiction of a state to the weirdly moralistic approach of California, which insists that a security not registered and approved by that state—and approval is not easy to come by—is not a security at all! Meaning that it will not be enforced as a contract in that state. New York's Martin Act, which is more typical, prohibits fraudulent misrepresentation and such-like in the sale of securities and empowers the attorney general to investigate intimations of same. A major purpose of the state laws is to make certain that if an organization sells securities within the state, citizens of the state will be able to sue it there for theft-like activities.

So the issuance and exchange of corporate paper, whether debt or equity or mixed, is regulated according to a rather complex scheme. But this paper, whatever its symbolism, is just paper. You might say it is the "currency" of the American corporate system, of our productive machine. This system itself is also regulated as the actual institutional network that it really is. Let's take a brief look at what lies *behind* the paper.

We started out by asking the rather booming question, "What is a corporation?" We saw that it was a certain kind of legal form that made a great variety of legally enforceable promises to different people. All this, it should be noted, is abstract legal conception—and the law, it should be further noted, is no more and no less than courts make of it. But the plants and machines, along with the people who work them and run them, are there whatever the paper says or whatever the courts, helped by various governments, say it says. Whatever the paper may be, the people and things are real—and so are the products that roll off the production lines. This is dramatically clear when a corporation gets into great trouble and has to be "reorganized." This process involves a frantic reshuffling of paper—and in terms of paper and other legalities the reorganized corporation may end up very substantially altered—but the corporation as an organization of people and things is apt to remain quite unchanged both during and after. So at least half of the answer to the question, "What is a corporation?" must be that it is an institution. The paper part is only half the story. After all is done, the flood of legalities is nothing but a way of recognizing institutional existence. Corporations are real.

And they are not isolated realities but are all related in the overall framework of industry. To put it simply as a fact, big corporations are the American way of carrying on the business of industrial production. Indeed, as a nation we have devoted most of our effort for about 100 years to the creation and then the protection of this very impressive network of industrial-financial institutions. They—and the social organization which goes with them, which depends on them materially, and which provides their spiritual motive power—are, in a practical way, the American heritage.

For this reason, and for many other reasons in addition to the fact that the groups that control the major corporations do not "own" them, I find it very funny when conventionally unrealistic people refer to them as "private" business. The only thing that's private about them is that nobody owns them *including* the government. They are not "private" certainly in the sense that Adam Smith talked about private property—incidentally, he was against them. Corporate paper might be called private property, although we have just seen how much it, too, is regulated by public authority. But big corporations are private only in the sense that they are not divisions of the government.

Ours is a corporate economy, and the big corporations (including the financial ones) are the greatest centers of power and prestige. One of the big experts in this field, A. A. Berle, Jr., says the American corporate system is now "the highest concentration of economic power in recorded history"—the Russians haven't caught us yet. His figures are that, on an asset basis, 150 corporations account for 50 per cent of American manufacturing. And 500 of them own two-thirds of the country's productive assets, not counting agriculture. If you want detailed illustrations of this overall picture, thumb through the *Fortune* list sometime. (The sales of a half-dozen or so of the top corporations come to better than half of the federal government's revenue.)

Corporations are so very effective as a way of carrying on the business of industrialism because they are ways of organizing men, machines, and other wealth in large, purposeful agglomerations. If we ever found a way of organizing these organizations among themselves as each is organized in itself —and could do this without a dictatorship like the Soviets have and could do it before the Soviets or the Chinese pass us by—we would have the most powerful, productive, and long-to-live society mankind has ever known or imagined. We don't have that because the system as a whole is not well organized. But to put a long story in a short phrase, we have as good a system as we have because there exists in fact the necessary minimum amount of Organization of the Organizations. That is, there are some powerful regulators of the corporate system at work that, in effect, make the system work.

This regulation is very important to you as an investor because it keeps business going, it keeps recessions from deepening into depressions, and so on. Regulation of the corporate system is probably more important than the regulation of corporate paper, even to investors—on the theory that the Thing is always more important than the Sign of the Thing.

There are many naïve souls around who believe that corporate regulation begins and ends with the antitrust laws. But the antitrust laws are a pious joke—and the real regulation is not. Maybe "regulation" is not a big-enough word for what I am talking about. What I am really referring to is *assistance,* including regulation—and in some few cases direct control. (Of course when we really want to do business and no fooling around, as in wartime and other deep emergencies, we have a good number of direct controls.) For instance, various governments spend billions of dollars building roads: can you imagine any more crucial assistance-regulation for the automotive industry? Or take the aircraft, electronics, or nucleonics industries: where would they be today without the assistance-regulation represented by the billions of dollars of military procurement and other outright subsidy provided by the federal government as broker between the producing corporations and the working, taxpaying population? And during the great depression when the government boondoggled-out some considerable sums to the financially embarrassed customers of the great corporations, wasn't that the most important kind of immediate "regulation" needed by those corporations at that moment? We could even go back to the nineteenth century when the government made sure that the new railroad corporations would have enough land to build their railroads on.

We have never had the sort of free enterprise you read we

are losing, and we never will because it wouldn't work. The masters of government and the masters of economic enterprise are always the same people. When the main enterprise of the world was agricultural, the kings, the dukes, the knights, and the squires ran the country and supervised the farms. Just as a gang leader carries a switch blade and wears a tin jock strap, they carried swords and wore armor. And they had troubadors just as gang leaders have *West Side Story*. The knights and and the gangsters were and are more romantic than ordinary businessmen—but essentially both carried their weapons to do business, not to pose for artists. The rulers of Wall Street would jump into suits of armor too if that meant making a merger. The real big thing for men— no matter how it often looks otherwise—is successful economic functioning, just as the real big thing for women is the birth of a child. It has to be this way; this is life, and there is no escape from it, no way to die conveniently, no way to be born again and try it once more. But from this central necessity individuals can orbit at different distances, in different patterns, and at different speeds. The sin of conventional thinking is not that the conventions themselves are wrong— especially the big conventions relating to sex and children— but that it seeks to simplify the pattern of the orbit. Thus what we call free enterprise is one of a number of practical systems of economic functioning. In Russia the big businessmen are called commissars and they are also the rulers of the country. The Russians have now gotten used to their orbit— and we are used to ours.

The two greatest forms of assistance-regulation currently are the two sides of the federal budget—government taxation and spending. Government spending accounts for something under a fifth of the national product. The provisions of the Tax Code are probably the most powerful means of control ever exercised as a normal thing in a democratic society. Military spending—usually half or better of all federal spending—includes tens of thousands of items, all the way from supporting the zipper and hamburger markets to the most expensive and speculative type of scientific research. The government's research and development expenditures have created or vitally stimulated new industries and are responsible for myriads of new products (on which our growth is so dependent). On the other side, taxes have had a much more profound effect than is generally recognized in shaping—and thus regulating, whether or not consciously—our business development. A big example: the new pattern of tax mergers, creating diversified monsters which are put together more for financial than industrial purposes. Another big example: stimulation of plant expansion through liberalized depreciation allowances. Then there is the stimulation of speculative enterprises by taxes. A little example: the Broadway theater —which would not be anything recognizably like it is were it not for the expense-account trade in front of the footlights and the 90-per-cent money underwriting activities behind the footlights. (Speculate sometime on what $5,000,000,000 of expense-account money means to us socially—restaurant living, alcohol consumption, broad levels of middle-range employees getting a premature taste of high life, and so on.)

But spending and taxing, while the biggest, are not the only forms of government regulation of the nation's corporate business. Not by a long shot. There is the Federal Reserve Board's money and credit maneuvering—the one generally accepted form of national planning. Then there are all those alphabet agencies in Washington which, even though they are run by or with the close "co-operation" of industry representatives, still amount at least to a significant form of self-regulation. (Most of these, incidentally, are based and operate on a philosophy contrary to that of the antitrust laws; their enabling statutes frequently contain antitrust exemptions; and the administrative agencies all too often come into open conflict with the noble warrior-priests of the Justice Department who are entrusted with the high duty of preserving the flame in the holy lamp of Free Enterprise.) The major extent to which the Agriculture Department controls American agriculture, which probably could not otherwise survive, is too well known to require elaboration. As a matter of fact, all of these things are "well known"—what's missing is the general realization that all of them together constitute a *pattern*, a system of regulation. They were adopted one by one, as measures of expediency, and too many of us consequently still tend to see each in isolation. That's a mistake—especially since we owe so much of our prosperity to this existing regulation, and so much of the promise of progress to more and better regulation in the future. To comprehend the facts of the corporate system you have to be able to see not just each separate corporation but also the threads of connection between them.

Well, who runs this system in which we invest not only our savings but also our future national existence? When it was a-building, this impossible question was "easy" to answer —Rockefeller and Morgan ran it. Vanderbilt and Astor ran it, the Carnegies, Mellons, and so on ran it. Why? Because they "owned" so much of it. In the beginning, when you thought of the biggest things in business, you thought of individuals like these; today you think of corporations like G.M., A.T.&T., Metropolitan and Prudential, Sears Roebuck, the Pennsylvania Railroad, and so on. What happened to the fabled "captains of industry" and all their wealth? The wealth is still around—there are a few billionaire individuals and a good many more multi-billionaire family groups and a literal mob of multi-millionaires. While there are no definite statistics, it seems likely that a million individuals (or less) own a quarter or a third (or more) of all the corporate paper. And most of the remainder is held by that amorphous but very comfortable group called "the upper middle class." But very few of these people participate much in the running of the system—*as owners*.

The system is run by a group who are called, and increasingly are willing to be called, "the managers." They are becoming more and more professionalized, the national shrine being the Harvard School of Business. They run the corporations but they don't own them. At first blush that statement has a sad, wistful tone to it. But shed no tears for them. While exercising the greatest power in the nation, they are not going hungry—for anything. They get top salaries, bonuses, deferred compensation, pensions, expense accounts, long-term contracts, etc., etc. And it isn't as if they didn't own anything at all: I refer obliquely to stock options. For instance, at Ford the executives have received options in the past five years for stock worth more than $100,000,000 over the option price. One of the important executives had made or stands to make over $3,000,000 after taxes on his stock options—besides his base salary of $185,000. But $3,000,000 of stock is not especially noticeable in reference to the *ownership* of the Ford Motor Company. (It's nice, though, for the executive.)

And with the next question—Who elected the managers?— we come full circle round to our beginning point concerning the legalities of the corporate form and the significance (or lack of it) attaching to the stockholder's vote. *They elected themselves*. As a group they are the heirs of the dominant creators of the great family fortunes (Andrew Carnegie selected the guy who selected the guy who tapped Benjamin Fairless who gave the nod to Roger Blough: maybe) but now they are more or less in business for themselves. Moreover, they are sufficiently professionalized so that they move around with increasing ease among the top jobs in different corporations in widely separated industries. The top executive of the Defense Department—the biggest purchasing agency in the country—is just as easily the chief of the biggest automotive company or a major soap producer. The *fact* that they manage is more important than *what* they manage, because they are always managing the same thing— an institution, a mass of men working, a corporation. They manage men, so they are in effect politicians. But, of course, *private* politicians.

It's a wonderful system. More human than rational, less democratic than effective, but still for a while the biggest and best ever. The point I would like to emphasize is that corporations and the corporate system are not merely legal forms and rules but groups of men determined, like the rest of us, to live and prosper. And as they do, their promises— the stocks and bonds they issue as their currency, their open-end promises to pay—increase in value. At least as long as the system as such survives and functions. That is the outside limit: the healthy survival of the system itself. And here I would stress that the essential dynamic of the thing is that the system must be organized somewhat as the units are organized. Maybe ask yourself what Roger Blough would do if he was chairman of the Board of the United States and running it with the essential managerial approach with which he handles the United States Steel Corporation. Sounds awful, doesn't it? But that's the dynamic of the thing. There's one saving grace: if that were the case, and things went well democratically, we'd all be sassy, demanding steel workers making his executive life miserable.

The *inside* limit? Well, that's which corporation, when, for what price, and for how long.

CHAPTER ELEVEN

Management and the Investor

The management of Company X were going to make a mistake. They were about to buy a company because of its patents and processes. This company made a certain material which Company X needed for an important new product. There was no one else who made the material so the president and Company X's legal council were scheduled to take the jet the next day. They were taking a partner of an underwriting house with them too since they would need $500,000 to make the deal. This meant that they would have to sell more stock. They could easily do this since Wall Street rated them as a growth company and their stock was selling high. At lunch the president interviewed a young Ph.D. who was to be the scientist in charge of the new project. "Why do you pay a half million for them?" he asked. "They have no real patents—they have no know-how that I couldn't duplicate. Save your money. I'll make the material for you."

They hastily took another look at the patents. The young man was right—they hadn't researched the patents enough before—the young scientist showed them where they weren't basic. They went to the Coast and continued the negotiations but at the right time they said "you have no patents." The officers of the other company admitted this—their patents were superficial. The Company X people tried to buy the company for a much lower price but it was no deal. So they put the young Ph.D. to work. He fulfilled his promise. In less than a year he was not only turning out the same crucial material—it was much better.

Now the stockholders never knew all that happened. They were aware that the company passed through a rough period but the president assured them it was only temporary. Then things went better than ever; they thought their president was a hero—this company has great management they said.

Company X has courage and perception combined with recklessness—just a touch more recklessness could have wrecked it at various times, just a touch less courage would have tamed its growth and made it a much less dynamic organization—and its stockholders would have been much less wealthy. What is good management is just as subtle as what is good cooking. You know what it is by results—or do you? One would think that you did—but a lot of people don't really know good cooking when they eat it. That makes the situation even more complicated. It's true that if you want to become a good cook yourself you must have a natural love of taste—food must excite you and your mouth must for some reason be a sensitive instrument of experience. And you must be brought up in a milieu where the experience of the mouth is respected. There are a couple of countries where a great tradition of cooking has developed and where thousands of people are taught to cook well—so if good cooking is not necessarily rare one cannot say that good business management is necessarily rare either. However, even in these fortunate countries supremely good cooking is rare—and if by good management one means supremely capable or fortunate management, then the mysterious development of a human being and of the strange relationship of this human being to particular circumstances becomes the key to the problem and I don't know of any systematic way to look for the key. All I know is that if you look around you might find it.

Great management like a great football coach is the management that wins the most games. Obviously in this case the management had been sloppy in its patent research—it might, except for the luckiest sort of development, have saddled itself with a big new issue of stock for an acquisition that wasn't worth it. This would have diluted the equity of those stockholders who owned the company prior to the new financing. In other words, to make the deal the company would have had to ask for help from outsiders. This error might not have been fatal since no one else knew how easy it was to duplicate and improve on what the Coast company had. Later that year another company, a competitor of Company X, bought the Coast company. Even though this company—let's call it Company Z—had a mass of Ph.D.'s and prided itself on the large sums it spent on research, none of them understood how to do the trick or if they did they didn't succeed in convincing their president that they did. Actually Company Z research teams had tried for years to make this material but had never succeeded in making high-grade stuff. So the president of Company X was not so foolish in wanting the Coast company. If he had been more methodical in researching the patents he would have been less enthusiastic about the Coast company and he might have been content to buy the material for a while. That magic moment when he met the young Ph.D., who somehow knew the real answer to this problem, might not have occurred. So you can't say that the president of Company X was not a good manager—you can say he is not temperamentally methodical—but he may be temperamentally perceptive and courageous. After all, he bet—and bet heavily—on the young physicist. He didn't follow the cautious tactic that was open to him of buying the Coast company and seeing whether the young physicist could do it.

Only a few companies have championship management. One of the hopeful things about investing is that many companies are successfully run by assiduously working men of mediocre talents. Successful business management or investment, like the cooking found in some countries, does not depend on genius. Under many, though not all, circumstances, success is as natural in business as it is in gardening. Some people think you have to have a special green thumb to be a good gardener, but you don't. All you have to do is have good ground, good water, good weather, good seed, and read the instructions. You can even be a successful gardener with less than this.

When I planted my first garden, it was somewhat late for planting. I knew nothing about it. I had the idea that the onion sets and other seeds and plants had to be planted deep and sturdily so that they would have a good foundation to weather the storms. I found that I had done everything wrong. But the plants grew anyway. I learned that there is a force of life which has a will of its own and while this force can, of course, be greatly helped by intelligent management, it is our basic asset in any occupation and the basic reason why, with our ordinary powers, many of us may hope to do well.

This is also the reason why with the best managements there are times when a company or an investor won't do well, or may even go into a serious decline or even collapse. I learned this from gardening, too. Once when I had finally taken gardening more seriously, I planted some raspberry bushes. They did well for some years but then became blighted. There was no way, at that time, to cure them. This happens to business and products too. Management is, of course, extremely important. Like anyone who has seen the amazing results which can come from a combination of good circumstances and good management, I have a tremendous respect for its importance, but it is possible to overvalue management just as it is possible to overvalue anything else.

Or perhaps it is more accurate to say that it is possible to expect too much of management. What the investor wants from a management is, of course, the successful development of a company, but under some circumstances a management will be quite good if it keeps a company from going broke. President Romney of American Motors is undoubtedly one of the most brilliant business leaders the country has. When he first made compact cars the results were not so happy. The motorist was not ready to buy them yet. Moreover, when he first made them, the other car manufacturers were still turning out sensible-sized automobiles. Then they finally went too far and tried to sell the public trucks in car's clothing. Moreover, they didn't even make their expensive trucks well: 1956 to 1960 was a very sloppy period for the Detroit motor moguls. At the same time enough Americans gained experience with true sports cars and fell in love with this experience so that a mass market developed for smaller cars. Romney had probably entered the small-car market out of desperation—he had to do something to combat the enormous advertising of the big three. This was, of course, smart. Then luck came his way and he and his stockholders cashed in magnificently. But now luck is running out. Detroit has learned its lesson. General Motors and Ford are turning out smartly made, attractive, compact cars, and Romney with all his ability is up against a force which could put him back in his small and inconspicuous place again. Certainly Romney is now up against his toughest test—no matter how great he is. If the test is too tough, his stock

will go down, and when it goes down you won't hear many
in Wall Street saying enthusiastically what a great manager
he is. Still he was and, considering the circumstances, undoubtedly is. Another chance to show this may come his way
again some day.

Looking back now, I can remember moments when I
suddenly and penetratingly saw the symptoms of unusual
management and others when I suddenly saw the opposite.
In the latter case, this insight sadly revealed a previous error,
the error of thinking that the management had been unusually good. I cannot remember any moments of insight which
are wrong but I can remember moments of not having insight.

The Granite City Steel Company is now an important steel
producer, with a single plant located not far from the Mississippi River near St. Louis at Granite City, Illinois. When I
first knew it, it would have been classed as unimportant and
struggling. There was only one thing of unusual interest
about it—it was the only roller of flat rolled products west
of Chicago and east of the Rocky Mountains. With the marketing area of the Mississippi River Valley growing in an
obvious way, its geographic location was interesting. However, this also had disadvantages because ore had to be
hauled by rail rather than coming down by water as it did
to the various large Great Lake plants. No one rated Granite
City high because the huge mills in Chicago, even though
farther away from the Mississippi area, were more efficient
producers and could deliver at low cost through the canal and
river system to the St. Louis area. Everyone assumed that
when "things returned to normal," Granite City would have
rough sledding again.

Even so, I thought it was worthwhile to visit Granite City.
There, as assistant to its president and as head of its eco-

nomic and marketing research, I met Lillian Green. Lillian
is a very charming woman but it was not her charm which
made me think Granite City might be an unusual company.
It was the fact that the management was willing to hire a
woman to do serious work of an intellectual and policy-form-
ing nature which made me think it had a special quality.
Lillian had worked for Lehman Brothers, a prominent investment banking house, and had been assigned to the steel
section of the War Production Board, where the president of
Granite City had gotten to know her. She is an excellent
economist—well balanced, careful, a vigorous investigator,
and tenaciously true to the statistical implications of the
available facts.

I thought that when the president of the company brought
her back with him at the end of the war, it indicated an
unusual devotion to industrial truth on his part. And if truth
will deliver, as Chaucer said, then it was a good sign for
the company. Few steel companies then had fully qualified
economists advising their high commands, no small companies indulged themselves this way, and many small companies still don't think it worthwhile to buttress and verify
their planning by high-level economic investigation. Most
managements were still hostile to eggheads and believed
that thinking was for moments of relaxation. For a management to listen to a woman showed real probity because the
only value a woman's thought could have on economic sub-
jects would be its correctness. Nobody would like to hear
her think unless she was right.

Niedringhaus, the president, died the next year and my
big flash of intuition came when I met his successor, John
Marshall. It was one of those magic moments. Marshall was
a somewhat wispy man, his hands shook badly, usually he
would get off on some line of rather platitudinous thinking

which would not mark him as a man of unusual genius in any way. But that particular moment his power showed through.

I was ushered into his office and he was sitting down not behind his desk but in an upholstered, soft armchair which had an unbusiness-like prettiness because of its gay slipcover. I was in a rush and so was he. I asked him something about the company's plans for capital investment—one of the typical but crucial questions that security analysts ask. He said, and his thin hand waved elegantly with a lit cigarette in it, the way the hand of a rich man might wave elegantly at a cocktail party when he tells you he has bought another sports car—"We're thinking of spending $50,000,000 to $100,-000,000. Do you think that's a good idea?" One hundred million is no longer so much for the company but at that time, which is not very long ago, it was about five times as much as had been invested in its plant during its whole history. To spend that meant a change from the stature of real smallness to the stature of real industrial importance. I saw that despite his elegant, well-bred casualness, Marshall meant it. His smile was the sort of smile which well-bred Americans of his generation have when they are serious and confident.

The interview couldn't have lasted more than five minutes. I didn't ask him how he was going to finance this dream; it was enough for me that he had the dream. A management without dreams *cannot* be exceptional; a management with dreams *may* be foolish. One of the problems of analysis is to judge management dreams and there is no set way to do this. This was an occasion where I was present at a moment when the management was willing to tell me its dream and when I was correct in appraising the dream as being translatable into reality. In another mood Marshall might have been circumspect and I never would have caught the flash of knowledge and power which has changed the company (with Lillian's faithful assistance) from a very minor spot on the industrial map to one of the really well-thought-of investment situations.

A moment of revelation and intuition like this is, of course, most unusual. Granite City has turned out to be one of the outstanding investments in the steel industry and the case is closed on this particular bit of management analysis. If the question is asked, "Can unusual management capabilities be recognized in advance of their actual proof in the field of industry?" the answer is, yes. If one is asked, how often, I think the answer is, not often. Unusual management is unusual and, therefore, you are not likely to meet it often. In order to recognize it, you probably have to know something about the business being managed.

You have to have a feeling as to whether the management really knows what it is talking about, and to do this you must have acquired some feeling for the business yourself. There are quite a few bright, sincere people running businesses who say bright, inspiring things and yet they do not prove good managers.

Management capabilities are not abstract qualities; they are related to specific sorts of insight and even to specific moments of insight into specific opportunities. I think Marshall would have been no better than a fairly good president of a cosmetics company.

Business is an art. Just as some artists have unusual insight into sculpture and others into painting, and still others into music, so, too, some businessmen have insight into steel and others into medicine. There are also some areas of business where management can be shifted around but these are staff rather than leadership functions. For instance, the treasurer of a steel company could become a treasurer of an airline company. But such people may not really be businessmen. Instead they should be considered as highly skilled technicians of industry who can do a job as well in one place as another. The outstanding managers are people with the gift of insight into the personalities of a particular industry and such gifts are, by definition, unusual.

I think the key to understanding management is to realize it is not an abstract quality but related to particular opportunities. To recognize unusual management at an early date you must be aware yourself of some sort of unusual opportunity and then happen to meet someone in business who understands that opportunity. When I first visited Granite City Steel, I was prepared to be aware of the special opportunities of the area, since I had spent some years studying the steel business. I found a clue to something unusual in my first visit and this prepared me for the lucky moment of revelation when I met Marshall. Lillian took me aside later and told me more about Marshall.

His family had been involved in the steel fabricating business for a long while; he had been an engineer with Bethlehem Steel for many years before coming to be president of Granite City; his family interest, McClintock Marshall, had been sold out to Bethlehem Steel during the 1930's and Marshall was personally a man of great wealth with entree to the best banking circles. So I had a background on him which made me feel that he could do what he was dreaming of doing.

Marshall had not been an outstanding success with Bethlehem nor a failure. If you met the Bethlehem executives, you could understand why. Bethlehem people were all big, husky extroverts. They are men of vision too; in fact, a few years ago they were rated the top executive group of the industry.

But the hand of a Bethlehem executive never shakes; he doesn't have moods in which he can be either platitudinously pointless or suddenly intense, brilliant, incisive, and I imagine Marshall was pretty well suppressed at Bethlehem. Bethlehem already had all the vision, all the daring, and all the money that it required. Granite City needed exactly what Marshall had to offer.

One of the times I met good management and never knew it until later was with Dow Chemical. It was shortly after World War II. Security analysts were crawling out of New York to see what industry expected of the future. I was fairly new to professional analysis at that time and very new to on-the-spot field investigation, which is essential if there is to be an understanding of a new industry. The price of stocks had been depressed for so long by the aftermath of the great depression and the onslaught of war that security analysis could be done quite effectively from a library of manuals. The war had stopped the growth of companies, had created a scarcity of various goods, had interposed artificial prices, and had knocked down stock values. All that the analyst had to do was to imagine a new era of lower taxes, no controls, and any reasonable expansion of sales and profit margins. This easy desk chair imagining led to sound stock market conclusions so that grass roots investigation was not particularly necessary.

But the head of our research department was himself an enthusiastic investigator by temperament. He had been in a number of businesses before coming to Wall Street and had a vivid idea about what doesn't appear in the books. Under his leadership the firm developed a generous travel tradition and we were among the first of the major houses to put the sort of investment into field investigation which is now common and which is now essential for good security analysis.

The Dow Chemical Company had long been famous for good management when I met Willard Dow at the home office in Midland. I didn't appreciate then just how momentous and original some of its developments had been, but I was keenly aware that it was rated as one of the unusually well-run companies and I was curious to see what a well-managed company was like.

Midland is in a flat plain in central Michigan and you see the Dow plant sprouting from it the way a squirrel might see a large garden if he suddenly ran into a new backyard.

I was impressed with the main office since it was designed in gracious modern architecture. Willard Dow's brother, I had learned on the 30-mile drive from Bay City, was a modern architect and the landscape near Midland is filled with modern homes. At that time modern was new. There had hardly been any construction for five years and before the war people had still been dubious about modern architecture. The office building, both gracious and intelligent looking, confirmed what I had heard of the company.

When Willard Dow came out to greet me, he did not seem particularly modern. He didn't send his secretary but came himself as though to say, "This is not really a big business, I'm not really an important man, everything is really much smaller and more intimate." His very way of approaching me was sort of old-fashioned.

I sat talking with this important executive all morning and into the afternoon about all sorts of small things. He was a short man with a large head. His full head of white hair gave an air about him. The white hairs were strong and straight so that where the barber had cut them short on the side, they themselves looked slightly like a brush. It was a lot like chatting with a businessman in a small town. There's so much time to spare that you don't want to jeopardize it by getting down to business too quickly. As I listened to him I thought I was back in Newtown, Connecticut. I told Dow how his accent reminded me of our electrician and he said one of his ancestors had come from Fairfield County.

I frankly thought Dow was a little crazy in a mild, nice way, which was typical of some of the genteel, native people of Fairfield County. We had a simple lunch at the company cafeteria but sat at the special table of top executives. All that differentiates Dow top executives from Dow employees is a large, round table at one corner of the cafeteria. Dow introduced me to different eminent men—mostly chemists—and said I was from a brokerage house in New York.

They treated me seriously, asked me opinions as though I must have a lot of wisdom, and I tried to question them about the chemical business. Willard Dow asked me what kind of airplane, a DC–3 or a Lockheed Lodestar, I thought the company ought to buy. At that time I followed the aircraft industry and knew some bright young engineers in it. Passenger planes had also been retarded by the war. The industry was torn with debate as to whether it was wiser to concentrate on a modern twin-engine plane to take the place of the DC–3 or concentrate on a still better four-engine job than the DC–4.

My friends with American Airlines had urged Douglas to design a new twin-engine plane to take the place of the old workhorse. But Douglas, partly because of greatly underestimating the market for airline travel, refused. He tried to sell the industry on using war surplus DC–3's and buying its new DC–6. My friends, therefore, worked with Martin on a new twin-engine design and then switched to Consolidated Vultee to design the famous Convair. I was full of the lingo of the trade and the odd little details you get when you know people in business and Dow may have picked up something useful from me. Dow was, however, one of those New Englanders who likes to get others to talk, partly I think for amusement in the hopes that every now and then they will be a little silly. Anyone who has read the New England poetry of Robert Frost or Edward Arlington Robinson will know what I mean. The southern temperament likes to be heroic, but the New England temperament likes to see heroes wear themselves out. I think it was perhaps the pleasure that Dow got at seeing a Wall Street investigator toiling at trying to investigate that made him like me quite warmly.

Later the company bought a twin-engine Beechcraft and a couple of years later Dow was killed when it crashed in an icy storm. By then I knew that this mild, friendly, and eminent man liked me and I felt extremely upset and sad about his death. But despite this feeling of warmth I did not really appreciate that he was an industrial genius or, indeed, a genius of any sort.

I didn't understand this until much later, when I made a serious study of the chemical industry in preparation for my book, *Money Magic in Chemical Stocks,* which Forbes published in 1952. Other members of the Dow executive staff reflected their genius directly in their conversation, men like "Dutch" Beutel, who built and ran the giant Texas works, and Earl Bennett, who started with Dow's father at the foundation of the company and grew to be one of the most original and daring financial men any company has ever had. You could spot these men as industrial geniuses immediately. But Dow was opaque; you had to learn about him from his deeds; not even those who worked with him could convey the full force of his deeds.

When I understood more completely the history of the chemical industry, I began to understand through these deeds the quality of the man I had known. His deeds were an understanding of a certain type of opportunity—the opportunity and the vision both had to exist in order to create the remarkable accomplishment. The particular gift that Dow had was a very real, though extremely quiet, courage. During the depression most companies were forced to retreat—and some companies retreated even though they weren't forced to. But Dow saw he wasn't going to be forced back—he could even go ahead.

The products of Dow Chemical were in growing demand despite the general economic disaster—bromine, for example, was in greater demand than ever as an intermediate in the manufacture of the anti-knock fluid used in almost all gasolines. Ethyl gasoline was a new product then, and the use of ethyl fluid grew. The company didn't hesitate to exploit this opportunity because of general economic difficulties. Willard Dow said, "While the rest of the world was in very great depression, our people continued to be stimulated with the thought that there were new worlds to conquer, that the horizon was ever distant, and that there was an infinite amount of work for all if we could develop markets for a few new products."

In 1942 Dow and his warmhearted, hard-driving (and if you've been in an auto with him, you know this is meant literally) vice president, A. P. "Dutch" Beutel, looked over the flat gas- and oil-filled tidewater plains of Texas near Houston to locate their wartime-built Texas plant. Dow encouraged Beutel to buy up the countryside. Natural gas, suffering from lack of markets because new pipelines could not be built, was selling for two cents a thousand cubic feet. New gas wells were then a nuisance and drillers then prayed for oil. Natural gas, however, was something the company itself could use, both as a boiler fuel to generate electric power, which Dow needed in vast quantities to make chlorine, caustic soda, and magnesium, and to use for chemical synthesis. Dow and Beutel saw the great opportunity which cheap and temporarily unwanted natural gas opened up to them, and as I saw when "Dutch" took me around, they had become kings while they could. This gave Dow permanently low power costs and low-priced ethylene for its chemical synthesis.

One of my most interesting experiences with management analysis was with a company which is so closely indentified with a certain chemical that I cannot give its name. The company was not far from a century old when its specialized knowledge became of national value. For most of this time it had been a very small, family company, but some years before I got to know it well it had begun to grow.

The principal reason it had begun to grow was that in the late 1920's and early 1930's two young men joined its staff. I will call these men Ted and Jim. Ted started its research department and Jim joined later. Jim had a special fondness for this element, which then was virtually unused and certainly was unloved. Chemicals made from it are highly reactive and difficult to handle and also there was no likelihood that they would ever become cheap. It was hard to extract from the ore and high-grade ore was not at all plentiful. The basic chemical industry of the world is founded on common things like salt, coal, and petroleum which are plentiful and cheap.

Because of the success of the developments which were based on common, low-cost materials, it became one of the dogmas of marketing research that no product could amount to much if it were not based on cheap raw materials. But like all dogmas, something was overlooked—cheapness is not just a question of price; cheapness is also a question of function. A very rare and expensive thing may have strange and unusual powers of function which, under certain conditions, will make this strange rare thing very cheap. This seems to be happening today in the case of two extremely important metals, columbium and beryllium, and it has happened in the case of tantalum and silicon. These metals are so hard to extract from their ores that they sell in the $75-to-$2,000-a-pound range. Yet the demands of missiles and of nuclear power are so insistent that even at these high prices these metals may be cheap because they will open the way to very desirable achievements which are not possible without them.

The men who took an interest in various more unusual elements had years to wait before they had a commercial opportunity. But like all unusual people they had no regrets; they knew what they saw and what they understood. It was their fate to see things which others didn't, and because they saw great things, they eventually became great. Perhaps it was some strange quirk in their psyche, some unconscious rebellion against their fathers which enabled them to disregard the conventional point of view of the chemical industry and pay more attention to what was to be seen in the unusual elements.

Jim drank his martinis and waited for industry to get ready to use the unusual orbits in which the electrons of his element flowed. The company had some humdrum products to offer too. Jim was a good, even a delightful salesman. The years passed pleasantly and what he saw began to come true.

The years passed pleasantly for Ted, too, except that Ted is not such a relaxed person. During the war he was in the O.S.S. He parachuted into a Sicilian pasture, his mission being to radio what was going on in the fields above the beaches. A grenade exploded near him. When I met him a few years later, a black patch covered a missing eye and only one very intelligent blue eye remained of the pair which had founded the research department in 1928. I took an instant liking to Ted. Many fighting men are physically strong, they are brave, but you feel it is the bravery of a bull. Ted, who had a moderate build, had a delicate human bravery.

At the time I met him the extraordinary and long-kept secret possibilities of their special chemical love had not become important. Its possibilities in lubricants and plastics were, however, interesting and business was beginning to build in a quiet way. I could not figure where a very large increase of sales was coming from, but I had a very strong feeling about Ted and I took an interest in the company.

A year or so later the secret aspects became of world-shaking importance. The government gave the company a big contract and with the contract it built a large plant. When the plant was finally in operation, a small group of us devotees was taken down to see it. We had a long, delight-ful train ride, with bottles of fine, sour-mash sipping whisky as well as ordinary scotch and gin, and on the way we speculated as to how high the stock should go.

I had just been to an opening of the Egan Gallery where a number of my friends had their paintings. At the opening I had been happily uplifted by martinis and had promised a beautiful blonde named June Herman that I would buy one of her boy friend's paintings if the stock hit 75. It was then 45. She said, "How about a drawing if the stock hits 50?" June and I agreed on a drawing at 55 and a painting at 75. Later, on the way to the plant, with all of us sipping whisky, I told them the story of my promise. The stock had already gone through 55 and I had bought the drawing. We were all very happy that trip, especially on the way back after having seen the plant, and Ted impetuously said, "I'll take that obligation off your hands." I protested mildly, but he insisted, and since he had a great many times more stock than I and since I had done a good deal for the company through my various writings, I thought that was very nice of him and good for art too.

But as weeks went by Ted showed no signs of buying the picture. When June's boy friend had a one-man show, I reminded Ted. I told him that if he or his wife didn't like abstract art themselves, they could easily give it to a museum since the artist was one of the six best-rated abstractionists in America and he would not only be helping art but would get a tax deduction, but he never bought the painting.

I puzzled for a long while as to why he did not and decided that something had gone wrong psychologically. I sold my stock and tactfully got our clients out too. There was no rational reason why Ted should not have kept his word. He was a millionaire by then, the cost of the painting meant little to him, and he could have even gotten a generous tax credit. He had made the promise voluntarily in the presence of a full drawing room of friends and had made it with great deliberateness. He had every reason to want to please me in this very respectable way. But he couldn't bring himself to go through with it.

The government needed even more of the magic chemical and the company doubled its plant. Even though the new facilities were duplicates of the first, they had even more trouble with the second plant. Many of the same mistakes were made over again—the motors were not quite powerful enough, there was not enough emergency or stand-by equipment, throughout the new plant it was apparent that the decision had been to skimp. I could not but relate this fatal compulsion to underengineer, to hope to get by without adequate expenditure, to the failure to buy the painting. The difficulties with the first plant had seemed excusable because the plant was new, but the difficulties with the second could only be the result of some type of mismanagement. Looking back over the history of the company, I could see now that certain opportunities had been missed. I felt this was because of the inability of Ted to pay up. The company had had so many opportunities in new and rare chemicals that it had won anyway, and at the time the decisions which led to its missing some of the opportunities seemed wise because they were justified by its desire to concentrate on this certain nuclear element.

But after Ted's failure to fulfill his promise I reviewed the record of the company more critically and came to the conclusion that these other opportunities had been missed compulsively rather than rationally. Excellent as the record of the company had been, it could have been much more amazing since its research had been first in several very important areas of chemical metallurgy and the fact that they were first was attributable to a large extent to Ted's vision. But they hadn't exploited many of their opportunities.

At first it seemed, as Ted said, as though outside rivalries, the obtuseness of government agencies, the ruthless power of larger companies, the willingness of these larger companies to get into the business even at a sacrifice of profit was the reason for the company's failure to make the headway it should have made. At first I believed Ted's stories of outside adversities—but after my experience with the painting I began to suspect that the company's failure to develop as well as it might was traceable to some unsuspected, unanalyzed, inner compulsiveness of Ted's. Apparently these psychic forces did not operate adversely as long as a project was in the research stage. One of the odd things about the difficulties of the new plant was that the pilot plant had always operated very efficiently.

This often happens in the chemical industry when a company goes from pilot plant to a full-scale operation. The change in size is often accompanied by unexpected difficulties. But in this case and perhaps in many others the unexpected difficulties might not be quite so unexpected if the psychological make-up of the chief executives had been better understood by them. In this case an important reason for the failure of the larger plant was, as I have said, the failure to purchase large-enough or powerful-enough equipment or enough of it so that when something went wrong there was an immediate replacement.

In the pilot-plant operation this desire to get by with minimum expenditure had not been so important because the scale of operation was small. Since there are practical limits as to how small or low-powered the equipment you are buying can be, the pilot plant may have, by accident, been better engineered.

When it came to vision, Ted had it, he had an enthusiasm for new things and for getting information—this is what made him a valuable member of the Army's intelligence during the war. But when things became big scaled, other psychological forces apparently began to operate. Perhaps if the painter had been less famous or less of the *avant garde* of art, he would have been able to buy it. I of course do not really know what his compulsions were based on, but something deep flustered him and I have no doubt now that under certain conditions he is obsessed by them.

He has since been removed from active command of the company, having been given a more dignified but less responsible post and Jim is now in full charge. So far I have no clues to any important psychic difficulties in Jim. The faults of the plant have been remedied and the company is moving ahead, but I am not sure that a large percentage of the unusual opportunities which the company once had have not been permanently missed.

From the point of view of the average investor, the opportunity is probably more important than the management. This is because it is possible to recognize more good opportunities than good managements. There is a great deal of evidence about opportunities—the evidence is in balance sheets, in reports of earnings, articles in newspapers and magazines, in the experience of everyday life. People very often see clues to good investments in the products they buy—television and radio have undoubtedly led many people to buy the stock of Radio Corporation of America or Zenith. I.B.M. machines have convinced many businessmen to buy the stock of International Business Machines; Scotch tape was clue to a good investment in Minnesota Mining and Manufacturing; the common household plastics have inspired many investors to buy chemical stocks, etc.

Common experience with industry products or with published material about new products or services has also led to investment mistakes. Those who bought the stocks of radio and TV manufacturers might have struck it rich in Zenith or R.C.A. But they might also have struck it poor in Dumont which actually was the pioneer company in TV.

But to some extent opportunities make managements. Unless management is very lacking in business talent or very remiss in performance of its duties it should make something worthwhile, at least for a time, out of an unusual opportunity.

One of the odd things about the Ted and Jim situation was that there was a rival company which for years had struggled along as a distant second-best in the same field. Its management was not merely second-rate; it was sneered at throughout the investment world. Nothing the management ever said would happen did happen. But during those years there was very little real opportunity in this element anyway. Then the great opportunity came, the promoter who was so cordially disliked by Wall Street died; a more practical businessman was put in charge, he did what he said he would do, and the stock was more profitable to buy than that of Ted and Jim's company.

The average "outside" investor should pay a great deal of attention, therefore, to the observation of possible opportunities and should regard management as one of the imponderable factors which he has to accept as important but hopes he is lucky about. Of course there are always some people who know particular managements well—the salesmen selling to a company, the customers buying from it, the bankers, etc.—all these know the management of a particular company well and for this reason a reputation builds up and sometimes spreads widely among investors so that everyone practically knows that this or that company is well or badly managed. The trouble with these widespread reputations is that they eventually become exaggerated. Key people leave the company or get old but, even more important than that, the specific reasons why they were good come to an end. Management is, as I have said, partly related to the products of the company—and also partly to the general trend of the economy. The right men in the right place at the right time make a great company—they couldn't help it—but very often the right men remain after the time has gone, so then it's not so great—but then something changes among the men and the time changes too and it may be great again.

I think the conclusion is that if you are in a position to know management well then you should pay as much attention as you intelligently can to the management factor.

When you do this, you must honestly ask yourself: How good am I as a psychoanalyst? If you are not in a position to know much about the management or if you are not advised by someone who is in such a position and who also himself knows his business then the management factor, important as it can be, is something you may as well trust to luck about. The nature of life is such that there is a lot of luck to trust to.

CHAPTER TWELVE

How To Be Right About the Stock Market

Most people aren't surprised if they are wrong about the stock market. They know how to be wrong—it's a natural ability. They are suspicious, though, about anyone who says he knows how to be right. One thing they forget is that even they are not always wrong.

Being right about the market is not unreasonably difficult. It's possible, if you have a feeling for the market and enough experience, to be right the way a good ballplayer is right when he comes up to bat. Even the greatest batters never hit 1,000. People are too easily discouraged about the market; they expect too much of themselves.

In order to be right about the market you have to ask yourself, "What is the market trying to say?" Most people don't do this; they make up their minds what the market ought to do and then, when it does the opposite, they say that the market can't be understood. But the truth is they didn't try to understand it. This is really the main reason for their failure.

My way of understanding the market is on a discrepancy basis. This is somewhat the same way that a psychoanalyst tries to get a patient to understand himself. I have an idea, as everyone does, what the market ought to do. Like most human beings, my thoughts tend to be based on logic. I say to myself, "Business is good, it's making new records—the market ought to go up—or business is poor, getting worse, it ought to go down." Then I look at what the market is actually doing. Sometimes it acts logically and at other times it doesn't. Whatever it does, I try not to argue with it. For example, business is getting worse but the market is not going down. I don't say, "The market will go down tomorrow." Quite the contrary, it goes up a bit. If this discrepancy continues, I begin to think that the market is near or has reached its bottom and will begin to edge up—or if business is good and the market ceases to go up, I begin to think that the situation has become dangerous and the market will go down.

As I have said, this is somewhat the way the psychoanalyst finds out what a patient really thinks. The patient tries to explain himself to the analyst—he thinks he knows what's wrong with him; what he wants is for the analyst to cure him, but as the sessions wear on it becomes apparent that he didn't pay enough attention to all the thoughts that were going through his head. He selected those which he thought were logical and explained him to himself; he suppressed others which he had and which were undeniably real but which contradicted what he wanted to think. The analyst makes him aware of his suppressed thinking, brings these contradictions out, and with them he and the patient develop a better understanding of the problem.

To understand the market you should try to be as near as you can to what Freud said a psychoanalyst should be— a blank sheet of paper. You want to be written on by the market so you can read what the market says.

In my case, I had the naïve good luck in 1932 of guessing right and buying at the bottom. I think in anything you have to have a touch of beginner's luck or you don't begin. I also had a stroke of luck in 1933 when I read an article on Keynesian economics in an *avant garde* periodical. I am not by nature studious; I am just bright. If I were studious as well as bright, I would have been a great scholar long ago, but whenever I tried, the tedium of scholarship either wore me out or confused me. So I had to find a niche where bright perception paid and scholarship was not needed. This was in Wall Street. At any rate, the article on Keynesian economics pointed out you have to have an unbalanced national budget in order to have prosperity. Of course a national budget is not the same thing as a federal budget. Our federal government in Washington is only one of a large number of large and small government bodies which may or may not unbalance their budgets, and in addition to the aggregate in government budgets, the true national budget is made up of a host of personal and business budgets. At that time though, everyone was pretty broke and it was the federal government which had to take the lead in borrowing money and getting enterprise started. Since then the federal government has grown so huge that it has become doubtful that we can have prosperity without having an unbalanced Washington budget. They are still trying. Maybe they will find a way to encourage private enterprise sufficiently so that Washington can rest, but the point is that there has to be a collective urge or a single forceful source of enterprise, and this enterprise must take the practical form of someone borrowing and someone lending. I don't want to become a scholar and become tediously mixed up in explaining why this is. Maybe it isn't necessary, maybe you can see it intuitively as I did when I read the article in 1933. If you can't, perhaps one illustration will help: In every country of the world the population is rising. In order to take care of the larger population, production must be increased. This means new plants must be built, cities must be expanded, etc., etc. It takes time to do this and therefore there must be some way of lending money to finance the expansion. Now if the rise of population were temporary—if it were due to stop in 1970, let's say—the time might come when budgets didn't have to be unbalanced. In such a case there could be a closed, tight, balanced economic system. But the rise is continuous, so the borrowing and formation of new debt must be continuous too. It is the continuity of the problem that puzzles and frightens people: "How are we ever going to pay this back?" they say. They get worried about the national debt, consumer credit, state and municipal debts, etc., and then everyone tries to be thrifty and balance his budget. This always brings on bad business. I understood how this worked after I read this article, and when the Federal Reserve Board clamped down on credit in the spring of 1937, I sold a lot of stocks—I was pretty well out of the market when the crash came in the autumn.

In this case it wasn't the market I understood—it was economics. But the market acted logically and I was lucky. Naturally I expected it to keep on acting logically. I began to buy back after the crash but things got so bad in 1938 that I sold again. To my surprise the market began to go up. This was my first experience with what to many people seems the illogic of the market. Business got just about as bad in 1938 as it had been in 1932 but the market didn't get nearly so bad. The stocks that I had sold went up and I was in the very unhappy position of seeing all the advantage I had gained in 1937 lost.

This lesson of 1938 paid off in 1958. A severe recession had started in 1957 and continued into 1958. There was quite a lot of panic connected with it. Then one day there was a big sudden rally. Business was terrible, unemployment was at record levels, but the rally was spectacular. I felt the market had seen its bottom. I made a lot of money in 1958 simply because I understood the market—I knew what its contradiction meant. I also acquired a real reputation—my optimism stood out in Wall Street. This, I think, was my finest moment from the point of view of a pure understanding of the market. I had understood it in the summer of 1957 when business was booming and stocks had ceased to go up. I had large holdings of U.S. Steel and began to sell them. The company issued a magnificent report of its first half year of operation, but the stock got nowhere. I was in Provincetown on my vacation. It's good to have time to think. I wired my office, "This is an orange light." But I didn't say red light—so I can't say it was a great moment of aesthetic satisfaction. In 1958 I saw the green light clearly.

I saw things clearly too when the 1960 elections came up. I said in March of that year that Kennedy would win. Later I said it again in October and predicted a bull market. But I don't get the same aesthetic pleasure because Kennedy just squeaked in. I didn't appreciate the enormous power of the religious issue. I was lucky to be right—and, to some extent, understanding the market this time was a case of being right on politics. In 1949 I was right because I understood women —I knew they'd keep on buying, I figured they had enough money to stop the recession, and anyway Truman was in office—I knew he wouldn't hesitate to unbalance the budget. But in 1958 I completely understood the market.

When was I wrong? I was wrong in 1954. I argued with the market. I tried to be an economist instead of a market commentator. I felt Eisenhower's super-conservative policies would kill business, which they did. I was right about business—it went down; the market went up. The wealthy group who own most of the stocks and control 90 per cent of the buying power going into securities had tremendous emotional confidence in Eisenhower—he was their man, their party was in power, they thought they would do great things in the next few years, so they held what they owned and bought more. History shows they failed. When Eisenhower left office, unemployment was at record levels again, steel operations were the lowest in 22 years, but the wealthy group hadn't lost confidence in themselves—they still didn't want to sell their stocks. When Kennedy was elected they thought inflation might start again so they held them tighter.

A market is always made up of buyers and sellers—this is obvious, so obvious that it's easy to forget. In the stock market there are so many buyers and sellers that you very seldom know whom you are buying from or selling to. There are supposed to be 12,000,000 people owning publicly traded securities in the U.S.A. If, on the average, one per cent of these are interested in doing something on any particular day, this means that 120,000 people are either buying or selling, or maybe doing both. The individual is always dealing with this big abstraction—"they are doing this or they are doing that"—but "they" are just thousands of people like you— maybe wiser, maybe stupider, maybe better or worse informed—but no matter what, their money counts. And so does yours. But there are 119,999 of them and only one of you. Now let's suppose that suddenly every single one of these 119,999 people goes mad—they buy stocks, they scramble for them, they are like dope fiends taking the needle, they clamor, scream, and screech, they borrow and steal— what would you say? Since you don't know them, you do say, "They're going crazy"—you say, "The market is going crazy." This would be true. You, the only sane person in an insane world, would see this clearly—but what do you do?

The market goes crazy quite often, especially about certain stocks, then it gets sane, then it goes crazy again about something else. It's quite possible to feel that the market is crazy, but it's a mistake to think that it's not possible for it to stay that way. Market prices are the result of an extremely complex mixture of exaggerated hopes and fears, careful calculations, personal ambitions and problems, inside information, outside intuition, and inside and outside misinformation.

In the case of individual stocks some of the irrational forces can be so very strong that anything like a precise forecast of the action of a stock may prove impossible. Stocks constantly surprise me, usually pleasantly, because if you have a rational reason for owning a stock others eventually agree with you. But the moment of their agreement is very erratic—and then if they develop an irrational enthusiasm that's where you can make a lot of money if you don't argue. Understanding the market as a whole is more possible because the irrational forces cannot act so violently, no one has real inside information about the market as a whole—the situation is so huge that it becomes abstract and depersonalized and the market can be observed as a type of natural phenomenon. If you are interested in this sort of thing you gain a certain understanding of it. Even when you are wrong you still understand it—you just know you were wrong, you can see why.

As I said, prices are made up by those who want to sell versus those who want to buy. The market as a whole is so vast that ownership doesn't change much from day to day and the number of shares issued and outstanding in the hands of the public remains constant from day to day. There is a slow increase as companies sell additional stock or large holders unload some of their holdings but the day-to-day change is virtually nil and the change even over the course of a few years may be small. Therefore for practical purposes whoever wants to buy stock has to buy it from somebody who already owns it. The needs and moods of owners of stock therefore play a decisive role in deciding what the market does. If a true economic disaster has occurred, if tens of thousands of people are hard up, then they may have to sell their stocks. The buyers can take their time. Prices may go down to levels which are quite unreasonable, but they are real because people have to sell. As prices go down, thousands who don't have to sell may become scared, so they sell anyway. Then because of income taxes others start taking tax losses and this brings in a new supply of stock. So watching the tape you may see a constant tendency for stock to be supplied to whoever wants to buy it. You may notice that sales are at the bid side rather than on the offering side. Obviously if many sales are on the bid side it is the owners who are eager to sell. If many sales are on the offering side, it is the buyers who are eager to buy and this pushes a market up. But we are talking about a falling market—it falls until for some reason the owners of stock don't want to sell any more, or far fewer people do. The offerings dry up, the market ceases to go down—you seldom know why, you just observe that it happens. And the same is true when a market goes up. In this case, people for some reason, sensible or otherwise, are eager to buy. This enthusiastic spirit soon infects the owners of stock who become reluctant to sell and so there is less stock available and the buyers bid higher. You'll always find people less eager to sell when stocks go up and more eager to buy, and less eager to buy and more eager to sell when they go down. It's remarkably hard to get customers to take profits. But somehow, as a market rises, a growing number of people finally do become willing to part with their shares, and so when everything is booming and you think the market will go higher forever, it mysteriously begins to cease going higher. You can't be sure that later on the equation won't shift again—sellers will have sold enough and the market will go up some more. Markets go through periods of consolidation and then start on their way again. You can never be sure but you can take action in line with your observation. Gradually you find either that you were wrong, the halt was temporary, or that you were right and you adjust yourself to this new evidence as best you can. As I said, you can't bat 1,000—if you suspect that someone else can, you might as well give up, but if you realize that a mistake is not the same thing as a misunderstanding, you will find ways to be right on the market in a practical manner.

How do you rectify a mistake? In 1938 I realized I was wrong and simply bought back what I had sold. Can you be wrong twice—can you get "whipsawed"? You certainly can, it's happened to me. Because of the danger of this, professionals very often hesitate to make a second mistake—they recognize that they have been wrong and they "sweat it out." What you have to remember is that you never really buy the market—you buy particular stocks. The trend of the market is important because it represents the big forces which affect most companies, but there are always individual companies which are able to go against the trend. The organic chemical companies expanded in the early 1930's despite the depression, so did companies making vitamins; the wonder drugs began to be discovered about 1933—fortunes were made in such companies regardless of market conditions. The airplane industry expanded steadily throughout the 1930's— the railroad industry has gone downhill steadily since about 1925. One of the phrases I coined to get customers during slack times was, "It's always a good time to buy a good-enough stock." So if you have looked into a particular company carefully, and have really good reasons for thinking its stock is cheap, you have a pretty good chance of being right even if you are wrong about the market.

In 1954 when I was abysmally wrong about the market, I made money by concentrating on various nuclear stocks, especially lithium. I knew I was wrong about the market— I had to grin and bear it. I didn't have the guts to say so in so many words, so I changed gradually, but the nuclear stocks boomed. No one was shocked that I had guessed the market wrong. As I said, people expect to be wrong about it. What they don't realize is that they can also be right.